Savvy
DECISION
MAKING

Savvy
DECISION
MAKING

An Administrator's Guide to Using Focus Groups in Schools

Madhavi Jayanthi ▪ Janet S. Nelson

CORWIN PRESS, INC.
A Sage Publications Company
2455 Teller Road
Thousand Oaks, CA 91320-2218

E-mail: order@corwinpress.com
Call: (800) 818-7243 Fax: (800) 417-2466
www.corwinpress.com

For information:

Corwin Press, Inc.
A Sage Publications Company
2455 Teller Road
Thousand Oaks, California 91320
E-mail: order@corwinpress.com

Sage Publications Ltd.
6 Bonhill Street
London EC2A 4PU
United Kingdom

Sage Publications India Pvt. Ltd.
M-32 Market
Greater Kailash I
New Delhi 110 048 India

Printed in the United States of America

Library of Congress Cataloging-in-Publication Data

Jayanthi, Madhavi.
    Savvy decision making: An administrator's guide to using focus groups in schools / by Madhavi Jayanthi and Janet S. Nelson.
       p. cm.
    Includes bibliographical references and index.
    ISBN 0-7619-7818-6 (cloth) — ISBN 0-7619-7819-4 (pbk.)
    1. School management teams. 2. Focused group interviewing.
3. Group decision making.   I. Nelson, Janet S. II. Title.
    LB2806.3 J39 2001
    371.2—dc21   2001002712

This book is printed on acid-free paper.

01 02 03 04 05 06 07 7 6 5 4 3 2 1

Acquiring Editor:	Rachel Livsey
Corwin Editorial Assistant:	Phyllis Cappello
Production Editor:	Olivia Weber
Editorial Assistant:	Ester Marcelino
Typesetter/Designer:	Denyse Dunn
Cover Designer:	Tracy Miller
Copy Editor:	Carla Freeman

Contents

Preface

The need for this book became clear from our experiences as novices interested in the art of conducting focus groups. We remember the frustration and uncertainty we felt during our own attempts, nearly a decade ago, in learning how to plan and conduct focus groups. In recent years, we have watched in amazement the increased use of focus groups by schools and have been taken aback to learn that in some cases, focus groups have actually been misused. Granted, there are some good sources of information for someone who wants to know more about using focus groups. Unfortunately, almost all of these comprehensive sources are intended for researchers; none is directed specifically at school practitioners.

We wrote this book—a book that will help novice school practitioners conduct focus groups—to fulfill these deficiencies. We have based this book on two important sources of information: (a) an extensive review of literature and (b) our own experience as novices learning, the hard way, how to plan and conduct focus groups. Thus we have written the book we wish had been available when we were novices.

What is the purpose of this book?

Certainly, part of our purpose is for the readers to know more about focus groups, to know how focus groups might be used in schools, and to know how misuse of focus groups can be avoided. But our purpose goes beyond that: We want the readers to be able to actually use focus groups in ways that are practical and cost-effective *and* that will ensure the resulting information is accurate.

What are the key features of this book?

This "how-to" book is organized in a user-friendly manner to serve the needs of school practitioners. The key features of this book include the following:

- *Sequential Arrangement of Chapters:* The chapters in this book are not organized in a topical manner; instead, they are arranged sequentially to reflect the order of tasks necessary to plan and conduct a focus group project. In Figure A, this sequence of tasks has been explained by means of a flowchart.

- *Easy to Read:* The book is written in an informal style to enable the readers to grasp the information easily. We have distilled the available information on focus groups into straightforward explanations of what needs to be done and why.

- *Examples:* Several examples are included in each chapter to explain the variations and realities present in schools. These examples represent possible as well as actual uses of focus groups. In the case of the latter, the names of the schools, school districts, and people involved have been changed to maintain confidentiality. (However, in Chapter 1, we provide some examples of actual uses reported in the media: These examples are identifiable by means of the citations.)

- *Sample Material:* Samples of the forms, letters, lists, and all other materials that would be needed by the readers are included throughout this book. These samples can be modified as needed by the readers.

- *Main Points of the Chapter:* All the issues that would ever have to be considered while planning and preparing for the focus groups have been listed in the table of contents and at the beginning of each chapter in a question format. Readers will therefore not have to search the index or skim through the chapters to try to locate the desired information.

- *Reproducible Checklists:* Checklists that can be reproduced and used are included in this book. For instance, "At a Glance" checklists included at the end of the chapters summarize all the key activities that must be completed while planning and preparing for the focus groups.

- *FYI Boxes:* We present supporting information from the literature in FYI boxes. Although this information is not absolutely essential for learning how to do a particular task, it simply provides readers with additional helpful information.

- *Cross-Reference Boxes:* Information on related topics has been highlighted by means of cross-reference boxes. Again, this feature is designed to make the information in this book easily accessible.

What does each chapter cover?

There are four components to conducting a focus group: planning and decision making, recruiting, conducting a focus group, and analyzing and writing a report. In-depth guidelines for accomplishing each of these components are covered in this book.

In Chapter 1, we explain what a focus group is, discuss in general the ways schools can use focus groups, and make a case for using focus groups in schools. In Chapters 2, 3, 4, 5, and 6, we explain the first component

Figure A. A Flowchart of Tasks for Focus Group Projects

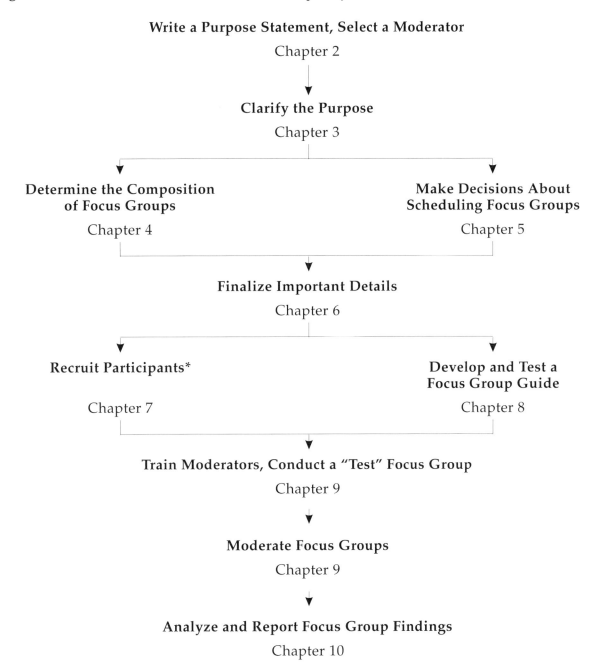

*This task may continue, overlapping with the next two tasks on the flowchart. That is, especially in a project with quite a few groups planned, you may still be recruiting some participants for the later groups as you are conducting the earlier groups.

—planning and decision-making activities—in depth. Chapter 2 specifically discusses guidelines for selecting a moderator early on in the focus group project. In Chapter 3, suggestions are given to guide the reader in the task of clarifying the purpose of the focus group project. In Chapter 4, guidelines are explained for determining which participants to include in the focus group project. In Chapter 5, strategies are discussed for guiding the reader with the task of scheduling focus groups (e.g., number of focus groups, location, or duration). Finally, in Chapter 6, the reader is alerted to all the remaining decisions that have to be made before participants can be recruited.

We explain the second component—recruiting participants—in Chapter 7. In this chapter, all the nuts and bolts of recruiting are explained. We explain the third component—conducting focus groups—in Chapters 8 and 9. Chapter 8 is specifically about preparing for the actual focus group, whereas Chapter 9 is about moderating a focus group. Finally, in Chapter 10, we explain the last component—analyzing and writing a report. The mechanics of analyzing the information gathered from the focus groups and writing a report of the findings are described. Instances in which analysis and reports are not needed are also described.

How should this book be used?

Many of the guidelines and activities expounded in this book are meant to help the reader conduct large focus group projects that will lead to high-stakes decisions. High-stakes decisions involve making changes that require enormous amounts of time, effort, and resources, and that affect many people. However, please note, there will be instances when some of the suggested activities may be unessential as well as impractical. This could happen, for instance, when one or two short focus groups are being considered for purposes that will not lead to high-stakes decisions. But obviously, when the stakes are high, we recommend that all the suggested activities be performed and all the cautionary notes be taken into account.

Acknowledgments

The contributions of the following reviewers are gratefully acknowledged:

Edie Holcomb
Education Director
Seattle Public Schools
Seattle, WA 98109

Daniel J. Gulchak
Complementing Education
Phoenix, AZ 85201

Rocky Killon
Assistant Superintendent
Lake Central School Corporation
St. John, IN 46373

Karen L. Tichy
Associate Superintendent for
    Instruction
Catholic Education Office
Archdiocese of St. Louis
St. Louis, MO 63108

Rose H. Weiss
Principal
Cambridge Academy
Pembroke Pines, FL 33029

About the Authors

Madhavi Jayanthi (MA-dh-vee Jay-YEN-thee) is a research consultant from Austin, Texas. She received her doctoral degree in Special Education from Northern Illinois University. Her varied professional experiences include teaching both children and adults with disabilities, teaching in institutions of higher education, and managing research projects. Her current research interests include decision-making processes in schools, effective and efficient classroom instructional practices, and effective use of student instructional time. She is now able to view these interests from "the other side of the desk" as her two children enter the public school system. Now based in Texas, she is originally from India.

Janet S. Nelson is Associate Professor of Curriculum, Instruction, and Special Education at the University of Southern Mississippi. She earned a doctoral degree in Educational Psychology, with a minor in Educational Administration, at Northern Illinois University, located in her hometown of DeKalb, Illinois. During her years as a classroom teacher, she held both general and special educator positions. That interest in general as well as special education programming now continues in her research. She is particularly interested in how students, families, and teachers view schooling, and how classroom teachers and researchers might work together to find practical ways to individualize instruction. She lives in Hattiesburg, Mississippi, with her husband. Her three adult sons live "up north"; she visits them as often as she can but never during the winter months.

We would like to dedicate this book to our families,
who patiently stood by us while we completed this project:

Mallika, Rohit, and Bindu
Dave, Vince, Matt, and Ben

1

Using Focus
Groups in Schools

Chapter at a Glance

- What is a focus group?
- What questions and decisions can focus groups address?
- What will schools gain by using focus groups?
- When should focus groups not be used?
- How can the focus group findings be used?
- What are the advantages and disadvantages of focus groups?

By all accounts, there has been a dramatic increase in the last decade in the number of schools using focus groups. A look at the popular media for the 1980s shows that there were virtually no reports of schools across the United States using focus groups for decision making. In the early 1990s, such reports began to appear and had quadrupled in number by the end of the decade (Nelson & Coe, 2000). This trend supports our strong belief that focus groups have an important role in schools.

But what is the role of focus groups in school decisions? We begin to answer that question in this chapter and continue to provide answers throughout the book. More specifically, the purpose of this first chapter is to define the term *focus group,* to discuss, in general, the ways schools can use them, and to provide some specific examples of their use by schools. We then make a case for using focus groups in schools and also explain when they should not be used. Finally, we explain how focus group findings can be used, as well as their advantages and disadvantages as information-gathering tools.

What Is a Focus Group?

If you have not used focus groups before, the term *focus group* may bring marketing or political campaigns to mind. You may be mentally picturing a group of ordinary citizens gathered together to express their opinions and perceptions about a product or a campaign issue. Based on this input, strategies for "selling" an idea or product will be developed. If you have this perception, you have some of the basics right. Typically, a focus group includes the following traits:

- Consists of 6 to 10 participants
- Is led by a trained moderator
- Has the purpose of discussing one topic or issue in depth

The term focus group refers to the role of the group members who are *focused* on a particular discussion topic. Certainly, such groups can provide you with information about people's opinions and feelings concerning the topic. But the real strength of focus groups is that you will also gain insight into their reasons for those opinions. In other words, you will understand the "Why?" behind their responses. Three aspects of focus groups help accomplish this. One, the open-ended questioning format of a focus group helps explore participants' comments. Two, there is an underlying assumption that participants are usually more willing to express their opinions amidst the security of other people who share some of their concerns and interests. And three, the atmosphere in focus groups is one of sharing and discussing rather than just interviewing, because moderators encourage participants to interact directly with each other. Thus the format of the group is conducive to gathering information not just about how people feel but also about why they feel that way. This is the essence of a focus group.

What Questions and Decisions Can Focus Groups Address?

As we discussed in the previous section, you can use focus groups to gather information about people's opinions, feelings, and perceptions. For example, you might want to know what they need, what they like and dislike, whether they are satisfied or dissatisfied, or what they believe are good solutions to a problem. In the first column of Table 1.1, we show some general categories of focus group use by schools. In the second column, for each

Table 1.1   Uses of Focus Groups by Schools

How Can Focus Groups Be Used?	Examples of Possible Uses	Examples of Actual Uses Reported in Media
To conduct needs assessment	To determine what technology training teachers believe is most important to address during inservice offerings	To determine what staff, faculty, higher education officials, parents, and students think high school graduates would need to succeed after graduation (Gerry, 2000)
Evaluation of overall institutional effectiveness	To determine perceived strengths, weaknesses, and/or overall effectiveness of school or district	To help assess the community's attitude toward the district in the face of funding concerns (Gaynair, 1995; Scruggs, 1994)
Evaluation of program/policy effectiveness	To determine consumer satisfaction (families, teachers, students) of the inclusion program and which aspects they regard as strong and weak	
To generate ideas	To generate ideas for developing public information campaign for an upcoming referendum (e.g., timing, media usage, etc.)	To find ways the school district can save money, improve management, and increase efficiency (Guerard, 2000)
Problem finding/definition	To determine whether there are problems in the transition from middle to high school and to determine the nature of any problems	To assess race relations in district high schools (Washington, 1994); to determine concerns regarding increasing enrollment and whether to seek another building referendum (Waller, 1995)
To generate solutions	To generate solutions for resolving communication problems that exist between home and school	
To change an existing program	To determine how to increase the number of people accessing the school Web site designed to provide information to students, parents, and the community	To restructure gifted programs and to find alternative funding ("Parents Look," 1993)
Budgeting decisions	To get feedback from the community regarding proposed budget priorities	To determine what the community wants from school and how much they will pay for it ("Focus Groups Planned," 1993)
Hiring decisions	To gather information about the skills that would be required to fill critical administrative positions	To get ideas on criteria for hiring a new superintendent (Chalifoux, 1997; "Post Falls Seeks Input," 2000)
Design/site new buildings	To generate ideas for the form and function of the "school building of the future"; to get feedback from the community regarding location and interior/exterior	To generate ideas for a new middle school (Campbell, 1992); to get community feedback on a facilities expansion plan (Bolton, 2000)
To test proposed plan or materials to learn about possible acceptance or rejection	To obtain community reaction toward a plan designed to enlist community support for a tax referendum; to test parent reaction to a new grade report form	To get public reaction to three different plans for reorganizing school boundaries (Russell, 1995); to determine whether or not to pursue a bond package plan (Berard, 1998)
Evaluation of training programs/materials	To determine whether teachers believe the inservice program is effective; to determine what new teachers think of the district's orientation and mentorship programs; to determine teacher opinions of the training materials for the newly adopted reading program	

(continued)

Table 1.1   Continued

How Can Focus Groups Be Used?	Examples of Possible Uses	Examples of Actual Uses Reported in Media
Evaluation of assessment methods	To determine whether the survey used to assess parent satisfaction asked all the important questions and whether the format was clear and convenient, to determine whether the district's minimum competency test for seniors achieves its purpose	
"Post mortems" of failed decisions	To determine people's reasons for voting against the referendum; to determine potential supporters' reasons for failing to vote	To understand why people opposed the referendum (Johnson, 1995)
Demonstration of accountability	To provide evidence to funding agencies that input was obtained from consumers (e.g., students, parents)	

of those general categories, we provide some examples of more specific possible uses. In the third column, we list some examples of reports in the media of schools actually using focus groups. A note about Table 1.1: We do not mean to imply that either the general categories of use or the possible and actual uses constitute exhaustive lists. In fact, we encourage you to consider the information we provide in Table 1.1—and in the examples we provide throughout the text—as a starting point for considering a whole range of other possible uses in your particular situation.

What Will Schools Gain by Using Focus Groups?

Given the examples of uses in this chapter as well as other possible uses you might consider, it is an understatement to say that focus groups can be used in many ways. For some of these uses—feedback on an inservice session, for example—focus group projects could be planned and conducted with little effort. However, in other cases—such as determining why district residents voted down a tax referendum—conducting focus groups would require a significant investment of resources. Why then should you invest the time and effort to learn about and conduct focus groups in schools? What will you gain? Here is our answer to these questions: to make consumer-supported decisions. As a school leader, you are probably all too aware that lack of support—for example, from teachers, parents, students, or the community—can turn a potentially successful decision into a failure. On the other hand, you also know that when you thoroughly understand relevant issues from the viewpoint of people directly affected by a decision, you are more likely to gain support and thereby ensure a successful outcome.

The importance of consumer support becomes critical when information is being gathered for *high-stakes* decisions. High-stakes decisions are those that affect many people or lead to changes requiring enormous amounts of time, effort, and resources. Examples of high-stakes decisions include deciding whether a school should be closed due to low enrollment, selecting a plan for changing school boundaries, determining whether a bond issue should be placed on the referendum, and selecting new curricula. In these cases, you would be wise to use focus groups to gather information from everyone who would be affected.

In addition to determining consumer support, another reason for conducting focus groups is to continually improve the effectiveness of school policies, programs, and products. For instance, you can use focus groups to get answers to questions such as "How can parent-teacher meetings better meet the needs of both parents and teachers?" "Are we making the best use of our time in our teacher meetings?" and "How can we improve the assignment book?" Another goal that is closely related to increasing effectiveness is increasing consumer use of such programs and products. Even if a program or product is inherently effective, successful implementation depends a great deal on whether consumers perceive it as both beneficial and feasible. Suppose, for example, that the assignment book mentioned above has been implemented schoolwide. Obviously, success depends on whether teachers and students actually use it. And in turn, use depends on whether they believe the assignment book will actually make a difference and whether it will be worth the trouble. Focus groups could give you an understanding of those teacher and student beliefs, which you could then use to improve the assignment book and to find ways to promote its use.

A final reason for using focus groups in schools is to enable school leaders to stay "in touch" with all those concerned (for example, teachers, parents, and students) on a routine basis. For instance, focus groups could be used to listen and attend to their needs, problems and concerns, likes and dislikes, and feelings of satisfaction and dissatisfaction. This information, although it may not be directly related to any particular decision currently being considered, can serve as important background information when particular decisions are on the table. Listening to consumer perceptions on a continuing basis has another powerful benefit: boosting morale. For example, we will never forget the comment of one parent as she left a focus group session we had conducted. As we profusely thanked the participants for their time, this parent said, with tears in her eyes, "Thank *you!* I'm just so glad to know that other parents are in the same boat, and that someone really listened to me tonight."

When Should Focus Groups Not Be Used?

Although there are several benefits in using focus groups across a broad range of applications, there are some instances in which focus groups should definitely not be used, and we discuss four of them here. Do *not* use focus groups in the following instances:

- You want information on a sensitive or intimate topic.
- You need information you can summarize numerically and use to make predictions about the opinions of others.
- Your purpose is for the group to resolve issues or solve problems.
- Your purpose is for the group to make a decision for you.

In the first instance, in which the topic is of a sensitive nature, it stands to reason that people would not be as inclined to be candid in a group as they might be in a one-on-one conversation. In the second instance, summarizing focus group information in a numerical form and making predictions on the basis of those numerical summaries is not appropriate. Focus group information can help you identify a range of opinions on a topic as well as understand reasons for those opinions. But the actual number of people in a focus group who express a particular view is not useful information because it is not an accurate indication of the proportion of people in the population who hold a similar view. For example, if every teacher in a focus group says the new reading program is a vast improvement over the previous program, you have no good reason to believe that 100% of the teachers in the district hold the same view. If you need numerical summaries, you will need to use another information-gathering tool, such as a survey.

The third instance in which focus groups should not be used is when the participants in a group are expected to resolve issues or solve problems by reaching a compromise or a consensus. Attaining a compromise or consensus is not feasible within the format and structure of a focus group. For example, focus group discussions are always conducted within a finite, predetermined amount of time. In other words, the focus group participants stop their discussions and go their own ways when the allotted time is over. On the other hand, if the goal is consensus or compromise, the participants in a group must have unlimited time and must be able to meet as many times as necessary to accomplish that goal. Therefore focus groups cannot be used for resolving issues or for solving problems. However, focus groups can be used to gather information that can be used toward resolving issues or, more specifically, to gather solutions to address the problems.

Finally, the fourth instance in which a focus group is not applicable is when you expect the participants in the group to have a decision ready for you. Remember, focus group participants cannot make decisions for you; they can only voice their feelings and opinions. The responsibility of making a decision ultimately rests on you.

How Can the Focus Group Findings Be Used?

To understand how focus groups findings can really be used in schools, it is first essential to address two questions. One, are focus group findings believable? In other words, are they valid? Two, can you make decisions on the basis of focus group findings alone? The answer to the first question is yes, focus group findings are believable and valid under three conditions: (a) when used appropriately and not misused, (b) when conducted properly, and (c) when interpreted correctly.

Before we answer the second question—can decisions be made on the basis of focus group findings alone?—consider the following example. If 18 out of 24 focus group participants (e.g., parents) indicate that an Individualized Education Plan (IEP) form is difficult to read, one cannot assume that 75% of the parents in a school would also find the form difficult. However, if a series of three focus groups reveal several problematic areas in the IEP forms, then it is possible to assume that these responses are also part of the perceptions of the target population. Thus although it is inappropriate to make a numerical projection from the findings, it is appropriate to assume that some of the information gathered will be manifested in the larger population.

Now, to come back to our question—can decisions be made on the basis of focus group findings alone? The answer is yes, they can, if the type of information obtained from a focus group is sufficient. On the other hand, you should not depend on such findings alone if you need numerical projections in addition to the information obtained from a focus group. In addition to the type of information desired, you should also consider the type of decision you are preparing to make. If you are planning on making some high-stakes decisions, you would be wise to base your decision on information from more than one source: Focus group information could provide important information but should be corroborated with information from other sources.

What Are the Advantages and Disadvantages of Focus Groups?

Like any information-gathering tool, focus groups have some advantages and disadvantages. In Table 1.2, we list nine issues that should be taken into account as well as advantages and disadvantages for each of those issues. In this section, we discuss two of those issues: the type of information gathered and flexibility.

Table 1.2   Advantages and Disadvantages of Focus Groups

	Advantages	*Disadvantages*
Flexibility	Focus groups are very flexible; there is no one correct way to use or implement them.	Flexibility may be interpreted as the freedom to plan, design, and conduct focus groups in a haphazard manner.
Face validity	Focus group findings have tremendous face validity—that is, what you see and hear is what you get. The information gathered from a focus group is therefore not difficult to understand.	
Cost	Costs can be contained if internal resources ("in-house moderators," free-of-cost meeting rooms) are used.	Focus groups can be expensive if external resources (moderators, meeting locations) must be used. However, the costs of large-scale survey projects are equally expensive.
Planning and preparation		Planning and preparing for a large focus group project takes time and effort; however, this time will be less than the time needed to interview all the focus group participants in-dividually. Also, this time may be comparable to the time taken to construct a good-quality survey instrument.
Type of information gathered	Focus groups have an advantage over surveys and brainstorming groups because only in a focus group is it possible to understand the "Why?" behind the participants' comments.	Unlike a survey, it is not possible to collect numerical information from a focus group.
Moderator reliance		The success of a focus group depends heavily on the skills of the moderator. If the moderator influences the discussion in any manner or form, the findings will be compromised.
Influence of the group processes	Focus groups provide a sense of anonymity and security for the participants, helping to facilitate candor in participants' comments. Focus groups stimulate the participants so that one person's comment triggers additional spontaneous comments from others.	Participants may sometimes not voice their real opinions and "go along" with what another participant said. However, what a moderator says and does during the focus group can diminish this possibility.
Direct contact with participants	Focus groups facilitate direct contact with the participants and help others to vicariously experience what the participants have experienced. Additional insights can also be obtained during a focus group by observing the participants' nonverbal behavior (e.g., expression of anger, the way participants handle a product being evaluated).	
Analyzing the findings	Information obtained from focus groups doesn't have to be subjected to sophisticated analysis methods like that from a survey.	Analyzing the information gathered from the focus group can be time-consuming and effort intensive depending on the method of analysis chosen.

With respect to the type of information that can be collected, focus groups have an advantage over surveys and brainstorming groups: Only in a focus group is it possible to understand the "Why?" behind participant comments. For instance, a survey response can be summarized as, "I like the curriculum a lot," whereas a focus group response can be summarized as, "I like the curriculum a lot because ____." Similarly, a comment from a brainstorming group could be summarized as, "We need more phones to solve this communication problem," but a focus group response could be summarized as, "We need more phones to solve this communication problem because ____. I believe that this will help because ____." These additional insights make the focus group a valuable tool.

The other issue, flexibility, holds both the promise of a major advantage and the danger of a common pitfall. Because there is no one correct way to implement focus groups, they are very flexible and have a wide range of uses. However, this very advantage will be a weakness if flexibility is interpreted as having the freedom to plan, design, and conduct focus groups in a haphazard manner. Doing so would surely weaken the results by compromising the quality, soundness, and trustworthiness of any information you obtain from the focus groups.

Although there are no hard-and-fast rules on how to conduct focus groups, some definite guidelines form a frame of reference and provide direction. In this book, we enumerate these guidelines, which are based on an extensive review of literature as well as our practical experience. You will then be able to make informed decisions and choices while planning, designing, and conducting focus groups. The goal of this book is not just to inform and educate you, but to guide you as you plan, design, and conduct focus groups.

2

Selecting a Moderator

Chapter at a Glance

- What is the moderator's role in the project?
- When should a moderator be chosen?
- Should an in-house moderator or an external moderator be used?
- Why are in-house moderators usually preferable to external moderators?
- Which in-house personnel can moderate a focus group?
- What specific criteria must be considered when selecting a moderator?
- When is an external moderator the appropriate choice?
- What qualities should one look for in an external moderator?

In this chapter, we make a case for two major recommendations. First, we demonstrate the importance of selecting the moderator early in the project, well before the focus groups are actually scheduled. Second, we argue that for most focus group projects in schools, in-house personnel are more practical and effective than external moderators.

What Is the Moderator's Role in the Project?

You may think of the moderator's role as being so obvious that no explanation is needed. Isn't the moderator's role as straightforward as the term implies, simply to *moderate* or guide the focus group discussion? In a word,

"No." The responsibilities of a moderator are not limited to the focus group discussion. Instead, the moderator's role begins well before and continues well after the focus group discussion. Before these discussions, the moderator may be responsible for designing and planning the focus groups, as well as for recruiting participants. After the discussions, the moderator may also analyze and summarize the findings and write any necessary reports. Given what we have said about this range of responsibilities, it would be hard to overstate the importance of the moderator's role in the project.

Of course, the degree to which the moderator alone is responsible for the completion of each of these responsibilities varies from project to project. But most often, the moderator is a project leader and may be the one person involved in every aspect of the project. Thus the role of the moderator is usually the most vital and essential component of the focus group project. The consistent involvement of the moderator often makes all the difference in whether you and others feel the group findings are accurate and trustworthy.

When Should a Moderator Be Chosen?

Given the significance of a moderator's role, it is essential that a moderator be selected early on, preferably at the very beginning of a focus group project. By doing so, the moderator will be able to take part in all the planning and decision-making processes. More important, this individual will be able to take part in the task of clarifying the purpose of the focus group project. This clarification process, discussed in the next chapter, involves fleshing out the rationale and the expected outcomes of the project so the goals and the objectives of the project are clear. By taking part in this process, the moderator will fully understand and grasp the real need for the project.

Awareness of and insight into the focus group project are not the only advantages of selecting a moderator early on. Here are some of the other advantages:

Cross-Reference Tip
To learn more about probing participants, please see Chapter 9, page 96.

- The moderator, by participating in all the planning and decision-making processes, helps ensure consistency within the project. Consistency becomes an absolute necessity when additional people are involved in the project. In such cases, the moderator may take on a supervisory role, ensuring that all personnel are implementing the procedures consistently.
- During the focus group, the moderator will be able to get the information that meets the goals and objectives of the project. The moderator's understanding of the real purpose of the focus group project is essential in knowing how to best *probe* participants. That is, the moderator will know when to ask participants to clarify or expand their comments, when to redirect participants to an aspect of the question not sufficiently explored, and so on.

- Throughout the project, the moderator will be able to judge whether the information being obtained from the participants is worthwhile and whether the issues of interest have been fully explored. That is, at some point, a moderator who fully understands the purpose of the project will realize that he or she is not hearing anything new: Participants' relevant comments have already been heard in focus groups held previously in the project.

In conclusion, much of the success of the project hinges on the moderator's role. To carry out that role effectively, the moderator needs to be involved almost from the beginning of the project.

Should an In-House Moderator or an External Moderator Be Used?

As we have emphasized, much of the success of your project depends on the moderator. Therefore all the decisions you make concerning moderators are extremely important. One such critical decision involves determining whether an in-house or an external moderator is needed. An external moderator, of course, is someone who is not an employee or a representative of your school or district. On the other hand, an in-house or internal moderator could be a teacher, a counselor, an administrator, or any other employee of the school. But *in-house* could also include any person whom the focus group participants believe acts on behalf of the school. Thus volunteers such as parent-teacher association officers and partners in education could be considered in-house if participants would perceive them as representatives of the school.

Write a Purpose Statement. Before you can make a good choice about in-house versus external moderators, you must first determine the purpose of the focus group project. This can be done simply by writing a phrase or a sentence that answers the question, "Why do I want to conduct focus groups?" For example, consider two districts that want to use focus groups to gather information about diversity programming. Their stated purposes, however, differ. The Balboa School Board, in the process of developing a districtwide program, states its purpose as, "To find out what people in the school and the community believe would make for an effective diversity program." The Martinville School Board, having had a diversity program in place for 3 years, wants "to know people's opinions about whether the diversity program has accomplished its purposes, which aspects of the program are most positive, and which aspects need to be changed."

Determine Whether the Purpose Is Evaluative. Once you have written a statement of the purpose of your project, you can then determine whether an in-house or an external moderator is needed. This decision is made on the basis of whether or not your stated purpose is evaluative in nature. By evaluative, we mean the appraisal of an existing school policy or program to determine its strengths, weaknesses, and overall value. If your purpose is not evaluative, you can choose an internal moderator. For example, an in-house moderator could be chosen in the Balboa School District project because they were planning a diversity program for the future. As discussed in the next section, there are many good reasons—not just affordability—that in-house moderators are the first choice for many focus projects in schools. However, using in-house moderators does not preclude using external moderators as needed. For example, if you don't have sufficient in-house personnel available, you can certainly contract for outside help to moderate some or all the focus groups.

In contrast, the Martinville School District could not choose an in-house moderator because they were evaluating a program that had been in place. Thus if your stated purpose is evaluative in nature, you have no choice: You must select an external moderator. In the presence of an external moderator, the participants may feel freer to voice their real opinions. On the contrary, if an in-house moderator is used, the participants might be inclined to say what they think the in-house moderator wants to hear and may avoid being critical of the institution the moderator represents. In the Martinville example, you can well imagine that if a representative of the school acted as moderator, participants in focus groups might not want to voice any criticisms of the diversity program the district had implemented 3 years ago.

It is important to note, though, that even when the purpose is evaluative, it is not necessary for in-house people to be uninvolved. Certainly, in-house personnel should not be involved in the actual focus group discussions. However, in-house personnel can and should work jointly with the external moderator in other aspects of the project.

Why Are In-House Moderators Usually Preferable to External Moderators?

The position that in-house moderators are preferable to external moderators represents a different point of view than the one held in the past. Previously, when public agencies such as schools wanted to conduct focus groups, the trend was to hire moderators from marketing research firms. However, this way of doing things carried with it the following problems:

- Hiring external moderators to conduct focus groups, even for one project, is an expensive proposition for most schools and school districts.

FYI: Shift in Perspective

Over the past decade, focus groups have taken on different roles in the public and non-profit sector. For a number of years, if you wanted to conduct focus groups, the only option available to public and non-profit organizations was to hire an outside expert. The outside expert would conduct the research, present the report, and move on. More recently, a new option has been successfully used in a variety of organizations. These public and non-profit organizations realized that study results are more likely to be successful if staff and others are actively involved in framing the problem, gathering the information, and preparing the report. . . . The model that has evolved has been a collaborative approach that places volunteers, staff members, and nonresearchers in the center of the focus group project. . . . Outside help, if and when needed, is provided on a consulting and contractual manner. (Krueger, 1994, p. 187)

- Schools may be tempted to limit costs by limiting the external moderator's role to conducting the focus groups and writing the reports. This would most certainly be false economy: Excluding the moderator from the planning phase would put the whole project at risk. As we pointed out earlier in this chapter, it is vital that the moderator be involved from the beginning of the project if the resulting information is to be of value.
- Although external moderators are knowledgeable in the art of moderating focus groups, their awareness of school-related issues and topics may be minimal.
- By being unfamiliar with the background of the participants taking part in the focus groups, external moderators may not truly understand the context of participants' comments. In other words, knowing "where the participants are coming from" is beneficial in understanding and interpreting their comments. The moderators may miss some nuances of participants' comments and thus may be unable to effectively probe the participants for added specificity and clarity.

In summary, our contention is that in-house personnel are best suited to moderate focus groups in school projects. These individuals can more easily be involved in the decision-making processes at the beginning and throughout the focus group project. By virtue of their early involvement in the project and their general knowledge of the school and community, they will be more aware of the subtleties of the issues surrounding the need for the project. Because of this understanding, in-house moderators will be in a better position to facilitate the gathering of information that is accurate as well as useful. Furthermore, because they have a vested interest in the accuracy of the focus group findings, they will be truly motivated to listen and to draw out all relevant information from participants. For these reasons, we recommend using in-house rather than external moderators whenever possible.

Which In-House Personnel Can Moderate a Focus Group?

Anyone in-house—whether an employee or a volunteer—can conduct a focus group if that person wishes to do so and is suited to the task. Although conducting focus groups is a skill that needs to be learned, it is not a task that is very difficult to master. People with the right skills and personality can be trained, or train themselves, to moderate a focus group. Observing others and practicing are two things that also help an individual become a good moderator. A good moderator is one who has the right personality traits and has gained a lot of practice and experience observing and conducting focus groups.

The first question you may be asking is, "Can I be the in-house person to conduct the focus groups?" The answer to that question requires you to look objectively at yourself. (This objective look would also apply to anyone else in-house you would consider a possible choice.) To get started, consider the statements in Form 2.1. If you answer "Yes" to all the items, then you have the characteristics required for learning to be a good moderator. But here is a note of caution: Answering yes to all the statements does not guarantee that you will make a great moderator. This process of self-questioning just tells you that you have the prerequisite skills. The absolute and ultimate test comes *after* the learning process: Whether you are a good moderator depends on your ability to actually conduct a focus group effectively and efficiently. As we mentioned earlier, these same "tests" and caveats apply to any other in-house person who might be a candidate for moderating focus groups.

What Specific Criteria Must Be Considered When Selecting a Moderator?

Cross-Reference Tip
To learn more about training moderators, please see Chapter 9, page 104.

Let's say you have gone through the foregoing process and decided there are several people who fulfill the general criteria for potential moderators. These people are both willing and able: They want to take on the task, they have good communication skills, they can take a neutral stance, they work well with others, and they carry out tasks in an organized and thorough manner. These people are suited to the task and, once trained, are likely to be effective moderators.

Form 2.1. Can I Conduct a Focus Group?

Willingness/Motivation

I want to conduct focus groups.	Yes	No
I am willing to listen and learn from the participants.	Yes	No
I have the motivation to learn how to moderate a focus group.	Yes	No
I am willing to work with others jointly.	Yes	No

Personality/Skills

I can communicate clearly and succinctly.	Yes	No
I am a good listener.	Yes	No
I am attentive to detail.	Yes	No
I am meticulous and fastidious.	Yes	No
I can be assertive but not dominating.	Yes	No
I can be unbiased and impartial.	Yes	No
I can set my own opinions aside and be open-minded.	Yes	No
I am sociable.	Yes	No
I can take constructive criticism.	Yes	No
I can work with others as a team member.	Yes	No

Now, you are ready to consider more specific criteria related to the particular focus group project you have in mind. You will need to consider two aspects of the project: the topic to be discussed in the focus group and the demographic characteristics of the potential participants. With respect to the focus group discussion topic, you will need to ascertain the level of the moderator's background knowledge. As we have pointed out earlier, the moderator's ability to effectively probe the participants depends in part on background knowledge. With respect to demographic characteristics, you will need to consider whether the characteristics of the moderator should be somewhat similar to those of the participants—for example, age, gender, or cultural background. All things being equal, when participants perceive a moderator to be someone like themselves, they are more likely to openly and honestly voice their opinions.

Similarity of moderators to participants, then, has an important advantage. But the disadvantage is that the selection process becomes more complicated. So, to what lengths should you go to ensure moderator-participant similarity? In general, our recommendation is to select moderators who are similar to the participants with respect to any demographic characteristics that are directly linked to the purpose of the focus groups. For instance, in our example of two school boards gathering information about diversity programming, cultural background *is* directly related in both cases to the purpose of the focus groups. Therefore when selecting a moderator for a focus group in such a project, it is essential to choose a moderator whose cultural background is similar to that of the participants.

When Is an External Moderator the Appropriate Choice?

Although an in-house moderator is preferable to an external moderator in most instances, an external moderator must be used whenever the purpose of a focus group project is evaluative in nature. As we discussed before, the presence of an in-house moderator may inhibit participants from making critical comments; thus some of the very information you are trying to obtain will be left unsaid. The following are some of the particular drawbacks of using in-house moderators for evaluative focus group projects:

- In-house moderators may approach a focus group having already come to some conclusions about the focus group topic. These preset notions may impair a moderator's ability to moderate effectively. For example, in-house moderators may not pick up on all aspects of participants' comments or may not probe for further depth when the comment is in conflict with their own views. This lack of objectivity may also be reflected in the manner in which findings are analyzed and reported.
- In-house moderators who are in a decision-making role may get defensive during the focus group when participants are critical of the school policies or practices. Consequently, the moderators may be unable to maintain a neutral stance and may be unable to probe participants' comments effectively.
- In-house moderators may be viewed as part of the problem. Participants may not be honest and blunt in the presence of moderators who are seen to represent the school in any way or form. This would be certainly true of school employees, especially those in positions of authority. It could also be true of people holding volunteer positions for the school if, as we discussed earlier, participants regard them as representatives of the school.

Therefore if your purpose is evaluative, participants need to feel free to do just that: evaluate, criticize, and find fault. Participants must be able to candidly share their real feelings and opinions and not just offer comments they believe will please the moderator. Furthermore, if the participants are employees of the school or school district, they should be able to talk openly without fear of repercussions from a superior. This candor can be achieved only when participants are completely assured of the confidentiality of their comments and have a moderator who is independent, impartial, and objective.

Table 2.1   What to Look for in an External Moderator

	Questions	*Tips/Comments*
Experience	How many focus groups have you conducted?	The candidate who has conducted the most focus groups is not necessarily the best candidate: Look for quality as well as quantity.
	Have you been in charge of a focus group project?	If you are looking for someone who can help and guide you in the planning and decision-making phase, select someone who has done those tasks before.
	Have you trained anyone in moderating a focus group?	If you are looking for someone who can assist you in moderating only, then someone with limited experience in supervision of projects will do.
Background knowledge	Have you conducted focus groups in schools?	If a candidate doesn't have experience with focus groups in schools, consider experience in other service agencies.
	What is your educational background?	Degrees in education are not necessary, but consider related fields.
References	Can you provide us with references?	Make sure you obtain contact information most useful for the particular individual (home or work telephone, e-mail).
	Can you provide us with samples of your work (e.g., audio or visual recordings, reports of focus groups results)?	Look for demonstration of specific moderating skills on audio or visual recordings. You can judge whether a candidate's experience is relevant to your project by the format and content of reports.
Charges	Do you charge by the hour or by the task?	If you're unfamiliar with focus group projects, compensation by the task may be more predictable.
	May I contract with you for designated services only?	Because the parameters of the project may change once the project is under way, make sure the contract covers this eventuality.
	What would be the total charges for the identified services?	Be realistic: Focus group professionals do not come cheap.

What Qualities Should One Look for in an External Moderator?

All that we have said earlier in this chapter about the characteristics of effective moderators applies to external as well as in-house moderators. The difference here is that you will not be assessing whether a candidate has the *prerequisites* to learn to be a good moderator; instead, you will be assessing whether the external candidate has already *acquired* the skills of moderating focus groups. If you should have an opportunity to observe the candidate actually conducting a focus group, by all means do so. But more likely, you will have to evaluate the candidate's moderating skills—and level of background knowledge relevant to your project—by interviewing the candidate and his or her references. Some possible questions to ask during interviews are listed in Table 2.1.

In this section, we have discussed what to look for in an external moderator. But we realize that you also need to know *where* to look. If you don't have any word-of-mouth recommendations from other educators, we suggest you look in the telephone directory Yellow Pages. In our areas, firms who conduct focus groups are listed under "Market Research & Analysis" and "Marketing Consultants." If you live in a rural area, you will be more likely to find listings in the telephone directory for the nearest metropolitan area. A worldwide directory of marketing research companies and services is also available on the Internet at: www.greenbook.org. It can be used to search for a moderator with specific qualifications, such as experience with children or in education.

We turn from the discussion of external moderators to reemphasize our premise stated earlier in this chapter: For most focus groups projects in schools, in-house moderators rather than external moderators are the best choice. In-house moderators are certainly more affordable and are more likely to be able to be involved at the beginning of the project. Therefore they will more completely understand the purpose of your particular project and will be able to couple that project-specific knowledge with more extensive background knowledge of educational issues in general.

At a Glance: Selecting a Moderator

❏ Have I written a statement about the project's purpose?
❏ Have I determined whether the project is evaluative in nature?
❏ Have I determined whether I need an in-house or an external moderator?

If an in-house moderator is needed,
❏ Have I determined who the in-house person will be?
❏ Have I determined whether I need to contract for outside expert help?
❏ Have I identified the external person?
❏ Have I interviewed and selected the expert?

If an external moderator is needed,
❏ Have I interviewed and selected the external moderator?
❏ Have I identified the in-house person who will be working with the external moderator?

3

Clarifying the Purpose

Chapter at a Glance

- Is the purpose of the project clear?
- What are the objectives of the project?
- What is the scope of the project?

Consider the following descriptions of school administrators who are planning to use focus groups.

Carol: How Not to Begin

Carol was an assistant principal in a middle school. She wanted to determine why only a few students with homework problems were using the after-school homework lab. After reflecting on the situation briefly, she summed up the need for the focus groups in terms of the following two issues: "What are the limitations of the after-school homework lab?" and "What can be done to improve the homework lab?"

John: A Better Way to Start Planning

John was the principal of a high school. He wanted to conduct some focus groups to determine how parents and students felt about school uniforms. He spent some time determining why these focus groups were necessary, asking himself a series of questions: "Why should I do these focus groups?"

"What do I expect to gain from these focus groups?" "How will I use this information?" In short, he took the time to question himself on the need for this project and to understand, clarify, and reflect on his goals and objectives for the project.

Clarifying the purpose of the project is an extremely crucial task. The importance of this task and its effect on the success of the project are often underestimated or worse yet, this task may not be addressed at all. There is a tendency to rush forward with the project, as Carol did in the above example, without clearly identifying the purpose, objectives, and intended outcomes. In reality, clarifying the purpose is a task that requires a significant amount of reflection and introspection.

In the following section, suggestions for clarifying the purpose of the project are explained. As you go through the activities suggested in this chapter, please note that there is no one way to do them. Your answers to the questions and the objectives you finally identify are reflections of what you want out of your project. That might differ from what someone else would want from a similar project. For this reason, we strongly recommend that you go through the activities listed in this chapter with another person or persons. This will give you a broader picture of the issues being considered and enable you to better clarify the purpose of your project.

Is the Purpose of the Project Clear?

Cross-Reference Tips

To learn more about writing a purpose statement, please see Chapter 2, page 13.

To learn more about the importance of selecting a moderator prior to clarifying the purpose, please see Chapter 2, page 12.

You have already written a purpose statement and selected a moderator (as explained in Chapter 2). The goal now is to use that purpose statement as a springboard to (a) carefully think through your reasons for conducting focus groups and (b) spell out the expected outcomes. Your aim should be to leave no stone unturned as you make certain the purpose of the project is completely understandable, with no ambiguous aspects. You can precisely define the purpose of the project by considering the following two self-questioning activities.

The first questions to ask yourself are as follows:

- What is it that I want to learn?
- What will I gain by conducting these focus groups?
- What will I do with the information I learn?

For instance, consider Carol, the assistant principal, and her reason for wanting to conduct focus groups: to determine why only a few students were using the after-school homework lab. Carol should have clarified the purpose by asking herself the above questions. If she had done so, this is how she might have sounded:

- What is it I want to learn?

    I want to learn why the students who need the lab are not using it.
    I want to know what I can do to make them use it more often.
    I want to know whether the lab is not meeting their needs.
    I want to know whether they dislike something about the lab.
    I want to know how they perceive the lab.
    I want to know whether they will use the lab more often if I improve it to meet their needs.
    I want to know whether something else is preventing them from using the lab, such as transportation or home situations.

- What will I gain by conducting these focus groups? What is it that I do not know now that I will know later?

    I do not know now why they are not using the lab. By conducting focus groups, I will know their reasons for not using it.

- What will I do with the information I learn? How will I use it?

    I will use it to make changes so more students will use the lab.

The second activity involves asking yourself "Why?" until the question is exhausted (Wheatley & Flexner, 1988). For instance, again consider Carol. Using her purpose statement as a starting point—to determine why only a few students were using the after-school homework lab—Carol should have asked herself "Why?" After she had answered this, Carol should have continued questioning herself and answering her own questions until she had reached a self-evident answer that made further questions pointless. Thus Carol's conversation with herself might have gone something like this:

Why do I want to conduct focus groups? To determine why only a few students are using the after-school homework lab.

Why do I want to know why only a few students are using the after-school homework lab? Because I want to see whether there is anything I can do to make more students use it.

Why do I want more students to use it? Because I want the ones who really need it to use it.

Why should the needy ones use it? Because it will help them complete their homework accurately.

Why should they complete their homework accurately? Because it will help them be successful at school.

If you feel as though you are going in circles while you are clarifying the purpose, do not despair. That is the nature of the activity. You want to address the issue from all sides so you have a good, thorough understanding of the problem.

What Are the Objectives of the Project?

After clarifying the purpose of the project, the next step is to make of a list of the objectives for the project. This activity serves an important purpose. It ensures that you, as the individual interested in conducting the focus groups, have thought about what you really want to know. The objectives could be written in the form of statements or questions. It is essential that these questions are not the ones asked of participants during a focus group discussion. Instead, they are questions to be asked of the focus group results. The questions to be asked of focus group participants are referred to in this book as the main questions; their formulation is explained further in Chapter 8. The development of the objectives described in this chapter will later serve as a foundation for those questions.

In Carol's case, she would develop objectives consistent with her purpose of determining why only a few students were using the after-school homework lab. Her list of objectives could have read as follows:

1. What are the various reasons for students not using the after-school homework lab?
2. What are the limitations of the homework lab?
3. How do students feel about the homework lab?
4. How do students perceive the homework lab?
5. What is the role of external factors in students not using the homework lab?
6. What can be done to improve the homework lab?
7. What do successful students think of the usefulness of the homework lab?
8. What helps successful students in completing their homework?

Please note that your objectives may overlap with other objectives or may be subsets of other objectives. This is of no concern here because the goal is to identify and explicitly list all the issues that are important to you. This list of objectives may sometimes take the form of a wish list. In reality, you may not be able to address all the objectives mentioned in this list with your available resources.

Because Carol did not spend enough time analyzing the need for focus groups, she failed to delve into the relevant aspects of the project. If, however, Carol had spent the time and effort necessary to clarify the purpose of the project, she would not have missed taking into account issues such as the perceptions and feelings of students. Perhaps these factors may have been possible answers to the problem.

Clarifying John's Statement of Purpose

John's statement of purpose: I want to conduct some focus groups to determine how parents and students feel about school uniforms.

First Self-Questioning Activity

- What is it that I want to learn?

  I want to learn . . .
  > what parents and students think of school uniforms.
  > whether they are in favor or opposed to school uniforms.
  > whether style or color of uniform will influence their feelings.
  > whether they perceive school uniforms as beneficial or detrimental.
  > whether they believe school uniforms will address some of the
  > problems we have been facing here at school.

- What will I gain by conducting these focus groups? What is it that I do not know now that I will know later?

  I will know how school uniforms will be received by parents and students. I will know the reasons behind their positions.

- What will I do with the information I learn?

  I will use the information in determining what the next course of action should be—should we develop a plan to address parent and student concerns or should we go ahead and make school uniforms mandatory for a trial period.

Second Self-Questioning Activity

Why do I want to conduct focus groups? Because I want to know how students and parents feel about school uniforms.

Why do I want to know how they feel? Because I will know what they like or dislike about the school uniforms and why.

Why do I want to know what they like or dislike? Because it will help me understand the issue better. I will know how they feel. I will know why they feel that way.

Why do I want to understand the issue better? Because it will help me determine what I should do next.

(continued)

List of Objectives

1. How do parents and students perceive school uniforms?

2. How do parents and students feel about the school uniforms?

3. What are the reasons behind their feelings and perceptions?

4. Will color and style of uniform affect their attitudes?

5. What concerns and reservations do parents and students have?

6. What do they think is the relationship between existing school problems and school uniforms?

The Scope of My Project

At this point, I do not want to know about the actual color, style, and form of the school uniform. I know that I will not be gathering information about the number of parents or students who are in favor of or against school uniforms. I also realize that I will not come to know whether school uniforms will actually help me in resolving the problems at school.

What Is the Scope of the Project?

It is not sufficient to know what you want out of the focus group project. It is also necessary to determine what will *not* be addressed by the project. The task here is to ask yourself the following questions: "What is it that I do not want to learn?" and "What are the limitations of the project?" Consider Carol again. After reflecting on the purpose of her project, Carol might have made the following statements:

"I am not interested in shutting down the lab. I just want to keep it open and have more students use it, especially students who really need it. So right now, I am not interested in learning about other options that may help students with their homework problems. I realize that the last two objectives relating to successful students cannot be covered by the present project. If I want to address these issues, I will have to expand the scope of the project to include students without homework problems."

As you can see, Carol is beginning to move on to the next phase of the planning process, determining whom to include in the focus group project. That is, she has decided it is more important to know why students who need the lab do not use it than to know how successful students view the lab. Given these priorities, she probably needs to include students with homework problems, rather than successful students, in her focus groups. In the next chapter, we cover the issue of whom to include in focus groups.

At a Glance: Clarifying the Purpose

❏ Have I clarified the purpose of the project?
❏ Have I made a list of the objectives of the project?
❏ Have I determined the scope of the project?

4

Determining the Composition of Focus Groups

Chapter at a Glance

- Who should participate in the focus groups?
- What are the criteria for screening and selection?
- Why is it essential to have primary and secondary participant groups?

Consider the following descriptions of school administrators who are planning to use focus groups.

Ray: How Not to Make Decisions About Focus Group Composition

Ray was the chief education officer of a suburban school district.

The residents of this East Coast community included retirees and families with children.

Who?

Ray wanted to gauge attitudes toward a proposed property tax increase.

The district had scheduled a tax referendum for later in the year for construction of a new high school. Ray wanted to conduct some focus

Why?

groups to get a feel for residents' opinions. His ultimate goal was to identify and address the concerns and reservations of the individuals and to gather support for the property tax hike.

How?

He conducted eight focus groups with PTA members and other community members.

First, Ray conducted three focus groups with families recruited from active PTA members. Then, he conducted another five focus groups with community members selected from the telephone directory. Ray was heartened by the opinions he heard during these focus groups, which were mainly in favor of the property tax increase.

Decision?

A large-scale public information campaign was *not* necessary.

Ray reported to the school board that scarce district resources need *not* be reallocated for a public information campaign given the community support that already existed.

Result?

The referendum was overwhelmingly defeated.

Some district residents—the individuals Ray had included in his focus groups—did support the referendum. However, many more, including families who were not involved in the PTA and district residents who did not have telephones, voted against the tax increase. Ray lost his opportunity to understand the concerns of the entire community because he had neglected to include focus groups composed of people from these and other such segments of the community.

Maria: A Better Way to Make Decisions About Focus Group Composition

Who?

Maria was the principal of a public elementary school.

This West Coast school, located in an affluent area, was known for its high concentration of individuals with Asian American backgrounds. Many of the children attended private schools instead of the neighborhood public schools. Because of the school's low enrollment, it faced a possible shutdown.

Why?

Maria wanted to know why families were not satisfied with the public school.

She decided to conduct some focus groups to identify and resolve the concerns and problems of families who had opted out of the public schools.

How?

She conducted eight focus groups with families of current and former students.

Maria first systematically identified families from two lists: students currently attending the public school and students currently attending private schools who had been enrolled in the public school earlier. She then screened the identified families on the bases of cultural background and level of satisfaction with the public school. When Maria conducted the series of focus groups, she selected participants for each group that were somewhat similar in terms of cultural background and degree of satisfaction with the public school. For example, she conducted four sessions with families of students who attended private schools: two sessions with families from the Asian American community and two with families from the white American community.

Maria decided to launch a targeted community information campaign.   **Decision?**

Maria designed a campaign that specifically addressed the concerns identified by the focus group participants.

There was a small but significant increase in enrollment figures.   **Result?**

After the campaign was launched, Maria was able to document a reversal of the declining enrollment trend. She also provided evidence that the figures would continue to increase, having received more telephone calls from families considering enrollment in the public school. She also noted that, in general, the school now had a more visible role in the community.

Determining the composition of focus groups involves identifying, screening, and selecting participants for each group. This is another important step in the planning process for your project. Remember from the previous chapter that the importance of the first step, clarifying the purpose, is often underestimated. The same thing can be said about determining the composition of each focus group. Care must also be exercised here so the value and accuracy of information collected will not be compromised. In this chapter, guidelines for deciding how to identify, screen, and select participants are provided.

Who Should Participate in the Focus Groups?

After clarifying the purpose of the project, the next step is to determine who should participate in the focus groups. When using focus groups in schools, potential participants could be classified according to the following categories and subcategories:

- Consumers of schools
    Parents and other family members
    Students

- School-related personnel
    Teachers
    Administrators
    Other personnel (e.g., nurses, counselors, and aides)

- Other individuals from the community
    School board members
    Community business leaders
    Community at large

Each of the above subcategories could be considered a possible *participant group.* A participant group is a segment of the population with some shared characteristics whose input is needed for your particular project. That segment of the population could be defined more broadly or more narrowly depending on the purpose of your project. For example, you might need input only from teachers in general for your project; in this case, you are defining a participant group broadly. In another case, you might need to define more narrow segments of the population to hear from (a) elementary teachers as distinct from secondary teachers or (b) general education teachers as distinct from special education teachers.

So, your task is to decide which participant group or groups are appropriate for your project. This decision is made on the basis of the purpose of the project. For example, suppose a kindergarten teacher wants to conduct focus groups to obtain some ideas for the upcoming open house. Here, the purpose is very simple and straightforward, clearly denoting families of kindergarten students as the only participant group that need be included in the project. Also, consider a special education supervisor in charge of staff development. He wants to conduct a couple of focus groups to get ideas for a workshop to be offered to the special education teachers. Once again, the purpose is very simple and straightforward, indicating that the participant group would be special education teachers. Note that more than one focus group session can be held with participants drawn from the same participant group. That is, the special education supervisor might plan two focus groups, each composed of 8 individuals. However, the 16 individuals across two focus groups would be drawn from just one participant group, namely special education teachers.

We have described some focus group projects for which only one participant group is necessary. However, there may be times when the purpose of a project dictates that more than one participant group needs to be included. For example, imagine that a district superintendent wants to conduct focus groups to determine how the proposal for a year-round school is being received by all concerned. To get a good picture of the situation, the superintendent could conduct focus groups with several participant groups: families, students, general education teachers, and special education teachers. Or, consider the case of an elementary school principal in an impoverished neighborhood. The school is trying to raise some funds to expand their existing computer lab. The principal wants to conduct some focus groups to generate ideas for raising funds. In this case, she could conduct focus groups with any or all of the following participant groups: families, teachers, and individuals from the community at large.

What Are the Criteria for Screening and Selection?

After determining the participant groups for the focus group project, the next step is to determine the criteria for screening and selecting them. This is an essential step in the focus group planning process because all potential participants must be screened according to predetermined criteria. Once you actually carry out that screening process, as discussed in Chapter 7, the process will serve two purposes. One, it will prequalify the participants for the focus group project by judging their suitability according to the predetermined criteria. Two, the process will ensure homogeneity of focus group participants. In this section, we discuss how to wisely plan for the screening and selection process.

Participants should be screened for suitability and homogeneity according to three sets of criteria:

- Project-specific criteria
- Demographic criteria
- Exclusion

Project-Specific Criteria. Project-specific criteria differ from one focus group project to another. They are unique and distinct for each project. Project-specific criteria emerge and take form from the purpose of the project. For example, again consider Ray, the chief education officer who wanted to conduct some focus groups to get a feeling for the community attitude toward a proposed property tax increase. Ray's ultimate goal was to identify and address the concerns and reservations of the individuals and gather support for the property tax hike; thus his focus group participants should have included opponents of the referendum as well as supporters. As stated earlier, Ray's first mistake was in drawing participants only from actively involved families and from community members with telephones. Ray also made an error when he did not screen potential participants. He should have screened according to a project-specific screening criterion, namely support (or lack of it) for the property tax hike. In other words, Ray should have screened his participants into two groups: those who opposed the increase and those who supported it. He should then have conducted separate focus groups with those two groups.

FYI: Homogeneity Versus Heterogeneity in Focus Groups

Homogeneous groupings are touted in this book as being better than heterogeneous groupings. However, it is important to note that this view is supported by logic rather than by research data. The basic premise behind the logical support for homogeneous grouping is that participants will be able to talk and discuss with each other when they have many things in common. For instance, Erkut and Fields (1987) note that it is essential to have as much commonality in a group as possible. All participants must be on the same wavelength. This commonality in a group is expected to increase candor of participant responses, allow for liberal sharing of ideas and opinions, and encourage total participation on the part of all participants. On the other hand, a heterogeneous focus group is believed to result in "a sharply divided group [that] will degenerate into a debate between the assertive individuals from either side, with others nodding but contributing little" (Broom & Dozier, 1990, as cited in Grunig, 1990).

Although the available evidence favors homogeneous groupings in conducting focus groups, this does not mean there is no place for heterogeneous groupings. Rather, there are times when heterogeneity may help the discussion or the group dynamics—for example, when generating a variety of ideas or solutions or when a range of opinions or feelings on a topic of interest is needed.

Also reflect on Maria, the principal of a public school who faced a possible school shutdown if the enrollment figures were not raised. Because Maria wanted to know why families were dissatisfied with the public school, her project-specific screening criterion (for families of students currently enrolled in public school) was level of satisfaction. Thus she determined whether or not each family on that list was satisfied. On the basis of the screening process, she then selected families that were dissatisfied with the public school.

Demographic Criteria. Demographic criteria are typically not project specific. Rather, they should be considered before screening participants in any focus group project. Demographic criteria include the following relevant variables:

- Age
- Gender
- Education
- Cultural/ethnic background

- Social status
- Family life-cycle status

Although the above variables should at least be considered in all cases, participants need not actually be screened on all of them in every focus group project. Determining which demographic variables should be used for screening participants in a particular focus group project is a task that is, once again, guided by the purpose of the project. Let's go back to Ray, the chief education officer investigating the community attitude toward the proposed property tax hike. Because the life-cycle status of the family might have an important bearing on the vote, opinions from individuals who represent the entire community should be taken. For instance, Ray could conduct focus groups with individuals who have children in high school, middle school, and/or elementary school. He could also plan focus groups with individuals who do not have school-age children, such as those with younger or older children and those with no children at all. Furthermore, age might be a factor for Ray to consider. He may suspect that some individuals' votes could be influenced by how many years they are beyond childbearing years. Finally, if Ray's suburban community included individuals of varying socioeconomic levels, he would also have to factor this variable into the equation.

Now, consider again the reason that Maria, the principal of the school in an affluent area, wanted to conduct the focus groups: to learn why families were not satisfied with the public school. To get a good picture of the situation, she would have to address the concerns of families that represented a cross section of the families within the school boundaries. Remember that a high proportion of the school's students were Asian American. Therefore Maria needed to use cultural background as a demographic screening criterion to understand reasons across cultural groups for family dissatisfaction with the school. Maria might also have considered the effects of gender. For example, the level of involvement in schooling decisions may be different for fathers compared with mothers in her attendance area. Therefore Maria could have included focus groups of fathers as well as focus groups of mothers in her project.

Exclusion Criteria. Exclusion criteria, like demographic criteria, should be taken into account while screening participants in any focus group project. In this instance, however, the criteria are grounds for excluding individuals. Potential participants should be eliminated from consideration when their presence could negatively affect the accurate and free flow of ideas from other participants. Exclusion criteria include four participant characteristics:

- Being an expert on the topic of discussion
- Being an authority figure
- Having previous focus group experience

Cross-Reference Tip
To learn about what moderators can do to offset unwanted group dynamics or manage problem participants, please see Chapter 9, page 99.

FYI: The Gender Factor

Should you include both male and female participants in any one focus group? Experts differ, with some taking the view that it is acceptable to mix sexes when the discussion topic is not related to sexual stereotypes (Advertising Research Foundation, 1985). However, the majority opinion is that in most cases, it is best *not* to plan mixed-gender focus groups. The discussion may not be as free flowing, and it may be more difficult to ensure that all group members have an equal opportunity to be heard. These disadvantages may stem from the tendency of members of one gender to express their opinions as if the members of the other gender were their audience (Axelrod, 1975). Also, men may take a more assertive role than women in a mixed-gender discussion (Krueger, 1994). In addition to these disadvantages, mixed-gender focus groups may be especially problematic when the topic is personal (Wells, 1974), if the topic is experienced differently by each sex (Krueger, 1994), and if the participants are children and adolescents (Vaughn, Schumm, & Sinagub, 1996). Given these concerns, our recommendation is to plan same-gender focus groups in almost all cases.

- Being an acquaintance or friend of another participant

A participant who is an *expert on the topic of discussion* (compared with other focus group participants) should not be included in the focus group. Other participants may perceive an individual with more experience or education in a given topic to be an expert. For instance, Maria, the school principal, was facing a possible school shutdown due to low enrollment. While selecting the participants for her focus groups, she might have excluded family members who were university faculty if she believed the other participants would feel less confident in expressing their own opinions. For similar reasons, Ray should have excluded accountants from his groups because they could have been considered experts on the proposed tax referendum. A participant who is an expert on the topic of discussion (compared with other focus group participants) should not be included in the focus group.

A participant who is an *authority figure* for the other focus group participants should not be used in a focus group. Consider a school principal who wants to conduct focus groups to generate some ideas for improving attendance at his school. To achieve this purpose, he would want to hear ideas from parents as well as teachers. However, parents might regard teachers as authority figures and defer to them during discussions. Therefore the principal should not include teachers in the same focus group as parents. Likewise, he should exclude principals from groups composed of teachers so that teachers' ideas could be freely expressed.

FYI: Exclusion Criteria in Focus Groups

Being an Expert on the Focus Group Discussion Topic

Experts are people who are more knowledgeable than others on a given topic. This knowledge could be a result of education or experience. Participants who are experts are usually excluded from the focus group to maintain homogeneity of the group (Advertising Research Foundation, 1985). Having an expert in a group is believed to be detrimental to the cohesiveness and functionality of a group. For instance, experts may dominate the discussion, whereas other individuals in the focus groups may defer their opinions in the presence of the expert. It is essential to note that the effect of this exclusion criterion on the outcome of the focus group has not been studied.

Being an Authority Figure

An authority figure is an individual who is in a position of power and/or holds a higher rank than the rest of the participants in the focus group. Participants who are authority figures are usually excluded from the focus group (Erkut & Fields, 1987). An authority figure, like an expert, can affect the functionality of the focus group. The effect of this exclusion criterion on the outcome of the focus group has not been studied.

Having Previous Focus Group Experience

The literature on using participants with prior focus group experience is ambiguous. One position favors using only participants who have had no prior focus group exposure at all. Proponents of this position believe that participants with prior focus group experience are seen as "knowing the ropes and putting on a show." The other position notes that participants with prior experience have a more relaxed attitude than novice participants. This relaxed attitude helps to "break the ice" and facilitate group discussion. Hayward and Rose (1995) investigated this issue and concluded that there was no substantial difference in the content generated during a focus group by participants with and without prior experience. However, they noted that at some point, experience does become counterproductive: The experienced participant can become too relaxed and inattentive and may disregard the moderator and make unhelpful and even destructive comments.

Being an Acquaintance or Friend

Although some experts in the field believe that having acquaintances or friends in a focus group is detrimental to the focus group discussion, others feel that it may be an asset (Wells, 1974). For instance, ac-

(continued)

quaintanceship is believed to result in less candid conversation and more uniform opinions. Also, friends may talk only to each other and not to the whole group, limiting group dynamics and group productivity. On the other hand, some experts believe that the naturalness and ease of conversation among friends is an asset. Fern (1982) studied the issue of acquaintanceship to determine whether there was a difference in the amount of content generated during a focus group of strangers as compared with a group of acquaintances. However, the results of the study did not clearly support strangers over acquaintances or vice versa.

A participant with *prior focus group experience* does not necessarily have to be excluded. The decision to include or exclude a participant with prior focus group experience can be made by determining whether the previous experience would have a negative effect during the focus group. It is known that the degree of negative influence is directly proportional to number of focus groups a participant has attended. So, where does one draw the line? When is some experience too much experience? Our recommendation is to exclude participants who have participated in four or more focus groups in the last 2 years. For example, again consider the principal who wanted to increase attendance at his school. While screening potential participants for the focus groups, he found that one teacher had been a participant in two focus groups held the previous year. The principal included this teacher because she had participated in only two focus groups during the last 2 years.

An individual who is a *friend, colleague, or acquaintance* of another participant does not necessarily have to be excluded from the focus group. When focus groups are used within the framework of schools, the participants often tend to be students, families, teachers, administrators, and other individuals with vested interests in schools. Thus it is almost impossible to work with individuals who are not friends, colleagues, or acquaintances of each other. The decision about whether or not to include or exclude a participant on the basis of this exclusion criterion can be made by asking oneself the following questions:

- Is the purpose of the project such that friends, acquaintances, or colleagues should not be used in a focus group?
- Will having friends, colleagues, or acquaintances in a focus group hinder the outcome of the focus group project?

For instance, consider the kindergarten teacher who wanted feedback from families about the upcoming kindergarten open house. As she selected the participants for the first focus group session, she noted that two of the participants were Latino and were acquaintances. She decided to include both families in the session. She believed they would feel more comfortable and would thus express their opinions more openly. On the other hand, imagine if she had noticed that three of the possible participants of the second focus group were "PTA buddies" who had served together on several committees. She might then have decided to exclude two of these individuals if she believed that together they might dominate the discussion.

Why Is it Essential to Have Primary and Secondary Participant Groups?

In the previous sections, we have discussed making decisions about the participant groups and the criteria for screening and selection. Remember that determining who will participate depends on the purpose of the project. Sometimes, this decision is simple and straightforward—for example, when just one participant group is being considered, such as families only or teachers only. The decision is not so simple when more than one participant group needs to be included to achieve the purpose. At such times, it is important to consider resources as well as purpose when making this decision. Conducting focus groups with many participant groups might be unrealistic when time, effort, and fiscal resources are in short supply. In such cases, it is essential to prioritize participant groups so that focus groups can be conducted with only the most important participants. Therefore the next step is to determine who will be the primary and secondary participant groups.

Primary Participant Groups. The participants who are absolutely necessary for the project are those drawn from the primary participant group. These are participants who must be heard and cannot be eliminated from the pool of potential participants. Information collected from them is of the utmost importance because their input forms the essential core of the information that is desired.

Secondary Participant Groups. The participants who would add depth and breadth to the information collected but whose presence is not absolutely essential would be drawn from the secondary participant group or groups. Therefore if time and monetary constraints are an issue, these participants could probably be eliminated from the pool of potential participants.

Let's consider Ray, the chief education officer whose ultimate goal was the passage of the referendum on property tax increase. Because his objectives were to identify the concerns and reservations and build support, he needed to hear from an entire cross section of the community. The stakes were high, and it would have been in his best interest to identify almost all the possible participant groups as primary participant groups. Thus the primary participant groups in this case would have been individuals who had children in high school, middle school, and/or elementary school as well as retired individuals with older children. The secondary participant groups would then have been individuals who had younger children and those with no children at all.

Also consider Maria, the school principal who faced a possible school shutdown. Because Maria also had a lot at stake, she prudently identified a total of four primary participant groups. As shown in the box on pages 41 and 42, she identified two types of families with children in private schools (who had attended the public school in the past), one Asian American and one white American. She also identified two types of families with children in public school, one Asian American and one white American. Therefore she planned to draw participants from a total of four participant groups. Maria could also have identified some secondary participant groups: Information might have been obtained from teachers at the school, families of students who had always been enrolled in private schools, and/or families with children in the public school who were satisfied.

Now, reflect on the district superintendent who wanted to conduct focus groups to determine how the proposed plan for a year-round school was being received by those concerned. Because moving to a year-round schedule would be a major change, he wanted to hear from everyone who would be affected. Ideally, he should have invested enough time, effort, and fiscal resources to accomplish this. However, he was unable to do so because he had only limited resources available. Consequently, he decided that three participant groups—parents, general education teachers, and special education teachers—were most essential and would be the primary participant groups. He then identified students as the secondary participant group and would include them if additional resources became available.

Remember the elementary school principal who wanted to conduct focus groups to generate ideas for raising funds for a computer lab. She decided that none of the participant groups she identified—families, teachers, and other community members—took priority over another. Nonetheless, she decided to keep the costs down by initially conducting focus groups with only the teachers. Thus in this case, the primary participant groups are teachers and the secondary participant groups are families and other individuals from the community.

Also, suppose an assistant principal of a middle school wants to conduct focus groups to determine why only a few students use the after-school homework lab. She could select (a) students with homework problems and their families as the primary participant groups and (b) students with successful homework experiences as the secondary participant groups. Individuals from the primary participant group could provide answers about the problems associated with the homework lab and how these problems could be rectified. Individuals from the secondary participant group could provide additional perspectives on the same issue by discussing what they would consider to be an effective and efficient homework lab. If resources were especially limited, the assistant principal could designate only students with homework problems as the primary participant group. She would then designate the families of these students as the secondary participant

Maria's Planning Worksheet

(Remember that Maria was the principal of an elementary public school located in an affluent area with a high concentration of residents from Asian American backgrounds. Because so many residents sent their children to private schools, Maria's school faced a possible shutdown due to low enrollment.)

● What is the purpose?

To determine why families, especially those who have enrolled or might enroll their children in private schools, are not satisfied with the public school

● Who should participate in the focus groups?

Two lists will be used:
1. Families with students currently enrolled in the public school
2. Families, also living in the attendance area, with elementary-school-aged children who formerly attended the public school

Who will be chosen from these lists?
1. Families, both white American and Asian American, with children in the public school, who are somewhat dissatisfied
2. Families, both white American and Asian American, with children formerly enrolled in the public school, who were dissatisfied and enrolled their children elsewhere

What are the criteria for screening and selection?
1. Cultural background
2. Level of satisfaction with the public elementary school

What are the primary participant groups?
1. Asian American families, with children *currently* in the public school, who are somewhat dissatisfied
2. White American families, with children *currently* in the public school, who are somewhat dissatisfied
3. Asian American families, with children *formerly* enrolled in the public school, who were dissatisfied and enrolled their children elsewhere
4. White American families, with children *formerly* enrolled in the public school, who were dissatisfied and enrolled their children elsewhere

What are the secondary participant groups?
1. Asian American families of students who had always been enrolled in private schools (It might be possible to understand

(continued)

whether these families ever seriously considered the public school and if so, why they decided against it.)

2. White American families of students who had always been enrolled in private schools (same reason as above)

3. Asian American families, with children *currently* in the public school, who are very satisfied (It might be possible to find out the aspects of our school that lead to satisfaction.)

4. White American families, with children *currently* in the public school, who are very satisfied (same reason as above)

5. Teachers at our school

group. Therefore in reality, selection of participants will be guided by the purpose of the project as well as by fiscal and monetary resources.

In summary, it is imperative that focus groups be conducted with as many participant groups as possible when making a high-stakes decision. Stakes are high when considering major changes involving enormous amounts of time, effort, and resources and when making decisions affecting many people. On the other hand, it is reasonable to limit the focus group project to only the primary participant groups when the stakes are low. Low-stakes decisions include those concerning minor issues or those concerning changes that would not necessitate enormous amounts of effort or monetary resources. In these cases, being more stringent with time and resources is understandable.

As you have seen, determining the composition of each focus group involves a series of decisions. These decisions should be made with a thorough understanding of the purpose of your focus group project foremost in your mind. At the same time, your decisions need to be tempered with an awareness of the resources you can dedicate to the project. We suggest that you end this chapter by looking again at the example in the box on pages 41 and 42 to see how Maria might have traced the decision-making process for her project.

At a Glance: Determining the Composition of Focus Groups

❏ Have I determined who should participate in the focus groups?
❏ Have I determined criteria for screening and selecting participants?
❏ Have I identified project-specific criteria?
❏ Have I determined which demographic criteria are relevant to my project?
❏ Have I determined whether all exclusion criteria are relevant to my project?
❏ Have I identified the primary and secondary participant groups?

5

Making Decisions About Scheduling Focus Groups

Chapter at a Glance

- What is the appropriate size of a focus group?
- How many focus groups should be conducted?
- How many times should each focus group meet?
- How long should each focus group last?
- Should a break be taken during a focus group?
- Where should focus groups be held?
- How many focus groups should be scheduled per day?

Consider the following descriptions of school administrators who are planning to use focus groups.

Linda: How Not to Determine Scheduling

Linda is the new assistant superintendent for professional development of a large school district. She remembers her own negative opinions about the district inservice days when she was a classroom teacher. Now that she is in charge, Linda wants to improve the existing inservice training programs.

She decides to gather as many ideas for improvement as possible by conducting focus groups with the district teachers. She identifies four teacher participant groups according to the following grade levels: primary, intermediate, middle, and high. She also decides to include five teachers in each focus group. Finally, she decides that each focus group would be a half-day long.

Steve: A Better Way to Determine Scheduling

Steve is the superintendent of an urban school district that has just been released from a desegregation court order and is now considering a return to neighborhood schools. He wants to make sure that district administrators fully understand the perceptions of district residents before deciding whether the change should be made and if so, how to make this change. Given the importance of this decision, Steve has already decided that the participants must represent the entire community. Now, he is carefully planning the focus group project. For example, he is determining how many participants should be in each focus group. He decides that each focus group should include only about six individuals so those participating will have more opportunities to expand and clarify the ideas they express. Steve believes it is more important for district administrators to more deeply understand residents' ideas than it is for them to hear a lot of ideas.

Focus group scheduling issues such as group size, number of groups, or duration and location of groups may seem at first to be relatively minor topics requiring simple, straightforward answers. However, considerable forethought and careful planning is needed to make decisions about these scheduling matters because such decisions influence the quality of the information that results from focus groups. In this chapter, guidelines for making scheduling decisions are provided.

What Is the Appropriate Size of a Focus Group?

The task here is to determine the size of the focus group. In other words, how many participants should be present in each focus group? To accomplish this task, the following three questions will have to be addressed:

- What is the ideal size of the focus group?

FYI: Number of Participants in a Focus Group

How many participants should there be in a focus group? Although some experts recommend 10 to 12 participants, others suggest 8 participants. Some put the lower limit at 5, while others believe that 4, 5, or even 6 participants seem too few.

As with most things related to focus groups, there are no definite solutions, only educated best guesses. These best guesses can be made by reflecting on what is known (researched) and believed (trial-and-error-experience) about the desired number of participants in a focus group. For instance, what we know based on research by Fern (1982) is that fewer ideas are generated in focus groups with four participants than in focus groups with eight participants.

Also consider what some of the users in the field believe. Merton, Fiske, and Kendall (1956), for example, recommend that the focus group should not be so large that it becomes unwieldy and does not allow for adequate participation by most members. On the other hand, the group should not be so small that the amount of information you obtain is not much more than the amount you would have obtained in one-on-one interviews. These goals are typically best achieved in a focus group of about 10 to 12 persons. However, if the participants are very homogeneous, a focus group could have more than 12 persons. Furthermore, a larger group can be used when the interviewer is interested in a wider range of perspectives of the situation rather than intensive reports of depth responses. Still, regardless of the purpose, the group should not be so large that most of the participants become little more than an audience for the few who use the opportunity to speak their minds.

Erkut and Fields (1987) give guidelines along a similar vein and note that small groups are more workable when detailed comments are needed from the participants. However, when the goal is to elicit relatively simple, straightforward opinions, they believe large groups are useful.

A final source of advice is Levy (1979). In his opinion, the optimal size of a focus group is eight people; a focus group with four, five, or six participants is too small. Participants may feel exposed, put on the spot, or excessively pressed to participate. One or two willing individuals may do most of the talking. The discussion in a smaller group is especially vulnerable to the personalities and biases of the few and therefore may represent too narrow a consideration of the topic. On the other hand, 10 to 12 individuals seem too many. People will have to wait for their turn and will have fewer opportunities to respond to

(continued)

others' comments. The group may become fragmented (side conversations, frequent murmuring), and the moderator may have problems controlling the group.

Given the above range of opinions, we have addressed the issue of group size by first considering the purpose of the focus group. We have then presented guidelines within the parameters suggested by the literature.

- What is the maximum number of participants that could be included per focus group?
- What is the minimum number of participants needed to conduct a focus group?

These questions can be best answered by taking into account, once again, the purpose of the focus group project.

The purpose of any focus group can be broadly classified into one of the following two categories.

- **Depth.** When the purpose of a group is depth, the goal is to have the participants generate ideas that are detailed, profound, and deep. The emphasis here is not on the quantity of responses but on the depth of responses.
- **Quantity.** When the purpose of a focus group is quantity, the goal is to have the participants generate as many responses (ideas) as possible. The emphasis here is to have a greater number of ideas rather than fewer ideas that are more detailed.

Cross-Reference Tip
To learn about the actual mechanics of contacting and scheduling participants, please see Chapter 7, page 66.

When the purpose of a group could be best described as **Depth,** the ideal size of that group is six individuals and the maximum size is eight individuals. In other words, although a focus group with six participants represents the ideal group size, the purpose of these focus groups can also be achieved with as many as eight participants. In fact, eight individuals should be scheduled per group so the group size would still be close to the ideal even if some of the individuals scheduled for the group do not actually attend. Keep in mind, though, that everyone scheduled may actually attend. In those cases, the group would be very difficult to handle if you had scheduled more individuals than the number of participants you determined to be the maximum group size. So, err on the side of the ideal rather than on the side of maximum group size: A smaller group is better than a larger one because all the participants will have a chance to voice and discuss their opinions adequately. At the same time, do allow for some "no-shows" when scheduling.

For instance, consider Steve, the superintendent who wants to conduct focus groups to get input from the district residents on the possible return of the school district to neighborhood schools. Steve believes that he can ideally get the kind of in-depth information he wants with six participants; however, he considers eight workable. So, he schedules eight individuals for each focus group. Thus the group size will be appropriate for his purpose if all those who are scheduled come as well as if two or three cancel or don't show up. Steve might modify his decision, however, if he finds that no-shows are rare. In that case, he may decide to schedule only six or seven participants for each focus group to keep the group size smaller and closer to the ideal size.

On the other hand, when the purpose of a focus group could be best described as **Quantity,** then the ideal size of that group is 8 individuals and the maximum size is 10 individuals. In other words, even though a focus group with 8 participants represents the ideal group size, the purpose of these focus groups can certainly be achieved with as many as 10 participants. Again, consider these ideal and maximum numbers as you schedule participants. Also, consider the likelihood of no-shows. When the purpose of a group is quantity, err on the side of the maximum rather than on the side of ideal group size: A larger group is preferable to a smaller one because more ideas will be generated during the focus group. In this case, it is better to have a marginally larger group because the effects of no-shows during the discussions may be more pronounced for focus groups with a purpose of quantity rather than depth. Therefore you should ensure that you have scheduled a sufficient number of individuals given your estimation of the likelihood that some scheduled participants will not actually attend.

Now, again consider Linda, the assistant superintendent for professional development who wants to use focus groups to generate ideas for improving district inservice programs. Because her purpose was really quantity rather than depth, her plan to include 5 teachers in each focus group is well below the ideal size even if every scheduled teacher attends. A better plan would be to aim for a group size of about 9 to 10 teachers for each group. If she had given the decision more thought, Linda would have concluded that no-shows were unlikely in this situation because the focus groups were to be held during work hours. She then would have scheduled just 10 teachers for each group so the size would be manageable.

Finally, we come to an inescapable question: Can focus groups be conducted with as few as four participants? The answer is yes, it is possible. However, the conversation may drag, the focus group may end before the allotted time, and the quality and quantity of information collected may not be adequate. Consequently, another focus group may be needed. Still, although a focus group with four participants may not be desirable, it is possible. The decision about whether or not to conduct a focus group with as few as four participants will ultimately rest on the individual planning and conducting the focus groups.

How Many Focus Groups
Should Be Conducted?

Cross-Reference Tip
A participant
group (e.g., par-
ents, teachers, or
students) is a seg-
ment of the popu-
lation whose input
is needed for the
focus group project.
To learn more
about participant
groups, please see
Chapter 4, page 32.

The task here is to determine how many focus groups are needed for each participant group. For example, Linda, the assistant superintendent of professional development, decided that she needed to include four participant groups—teachers at primary, intermediate, middle school, and high school levels—in her efforts to generate ideas for improving her district's in-service program. But, she still needs to decide how many focus groups of primary teachers to conduct, how many of intermediate teachers, and so on. To make this decision, she should first consider what the ideal would be.

The Ideal. One rule of thumb suggests conducting focus groups until little or no new information is obtained from a focus group session. That is, at some point, almost all the ideas expressed during a session will have already been expressed during previous sessions. This point is usually reached after 3 to 4 focus groups per participant group. Sometimes, though, as many as 5 or 6 focus groups are needed before little new information is generated. Thus for Linda, the ideal might be a total of about 12 to16 focus groups, 4 for each of her teacher participant groups.

The Norm. Unfortunately, most school personnel do not work under ideal circumstances. Often, time and cost constraints limit what school personnel can accomplish. Consequently, there is a need for suggestions and approaches that are practical and feasible. With respect to focus group projects, this need for practicality often means that school personnel must consider conducting fewer focus groups than the ideal discussed above. It is not surprising, then, that another rule of thumb is to conduct at least two focus groups per participant group. This rule of thumb assumes that conducting two focus groups is better than conducting one because you are not limited by the information of just one focus group. Also, in some cases, conducting only one focus group carries the risk that it will turn out to be atypical. Thus conducting two groups would help in overcoming the limitations and risks associated with conducting one focus group. More important, conducting two focus groups would be more realistic and practical than the recommended ideal.

Before deciding to use fewer groups than the ideal, you must make sure that doing so will not compromise the accuracy and usefulness of the focus group information. Therefore you should carefully consider the following factors:

- Purpose and scope of the focus group project
- Amount of emphasis that is to be placed on the findings

- Cost and time constraints
- Size of the participant pool

For example, Steve's district is considering a change to neighborhood schools and will rely heavily on the focus group information in making a decision. Therefore this high level of reliance and emphasis on the focus group findings increases the risk associated with conducting fewer than the ideal number of focus groups per participant group. Furthermore, the purpose and scope of Steve's focus group project is far-reaching. The decision to redraw attendance boundaries would affect nearly every teacher and every family in the district and would be in place for years. Finally, the size of Steve's participant pool is huge, including potentially every resident, teacher, and administrator in the district. If he plans only a couple of focus groups per participant group, he cannot be reasonably certain that the findings will give him what he needs: a sense of the range of the perceptions typical for each participant group. To make matters worse, some of the information missing from the findings might be very important. Certainly, the stakes are so high in Steve's case that he would be wise to follow the recommendation for the ideal number of focus groups!

Linda, who is gathering ideas for improving her district's inservice programs, is in a different situation. Her respondent pool consists only of the district teaching staff. Also, she is under time limits because she wants to use the two inservice days to make plans for the current academic year. Finally, the scope of her project is fairly narrow: Inservice needs can and do change from year to year, so any changes she makes need not be set in stone. On the other hand, Linda would not want the focus group information to be so atypical as to lead her in the wrong direction entirely. Given all these factors, Linda might want to follow recommendations for the norm and plan two focus groups per participant group.

The Exception. Let's suppose that Linda wants to get some quick feedback on a new inservice session she is planning. In this case, one focus group will be sufficient because she is only interested in getting some pointers on how to make the inservice session better. Another reason that one focus group will suffice for Linda is that she will make no major decisions or changes on the basis of the information she hears at this group.

To sum up the determination of how many focus groups are needed per participant group, it is important to reflect on the considerations discussed above—the ideal, the norm, or the exception—before deciding which rule of thumb to use. Also, you might switch to another rule of thumb as your project evolves. For example, you might start with one focus group, decide to do another one, and after that, decide to do one more. You may also choose to broaden the scope of your project if you find that the participants of a focus group were more atypical than anticipated.

How Many Times Should
Each Focus Group Meet?

A focus group as an entity meets just once. However, at times, depending on the purpose of the project, individuals from a focus group may be selected to take part in another related project. Let's suppose that after conducting the focus groups, Linda, the assistant superintendent, has come up with many ideas for improving district inservice programs. After using this input to develop new inservice approaches, she might want to conduct another series of focus groups to get feedback on her new plan. For this new series, she might recruit and schedule some of the individuals who had participated in her previous focus group project. However, Linda will have to make sure that none of the focus groups from the new series match any of the focus groups from the old series with respect to participant composition.

In the case of Steve, the urban school superintendent, suppose that a decision was made in favor of the neighborhood school concept. He might then want to conduct some additional focus groups to generate ideas for developing a campaign to gain the support of the community. As in the previous example, some participants from his first series of focus groups might also be participants in the second series.

How Long Should
Each Focus Group Last?

A focus group can last anywhere from 20 minutes to 2 hours. Focus groups should definitely not be longer than 2 hours. A longer discussion will probably be unproductive. At that point, everyone—the moderator as well as participants—may be tired or bored. The duration of a focus group can be estimated by taking into account the purpose of the group.

Reflect again on Steve's school district, which was considering a return to neighborhood schools. Because the original purpose was to gain in-depth understanding of some complex issues, Steve should plan for groups lasting 1½ to 2 hours. However, if he were to conduct a second series of focus groups to generate ideas for a public information campaign, those groups might be scheduled for only 45 minutes to an hour. On the other hand, Linda's decision to schedule half-day-long focus groups was not a good decision. Focus groups for any purpose are not likely to be very productive after 2 hours have passed. Furthermore, because the purpose of Linda's focus group was to elicit suggestions for improvement, a much shorter focus group—45 minutes to an hour—would be advisable. To take

Linda's case further, let's suppose that at some point in the overall planning process, she were to determine possible inservice topics. She might then hold some very brief focus groups, lasting only 20 to 30 minutes, to get some quick feedback on the usefulness of these topics.

Should a Break Be Taken During a Focus Group?

A break is not necessary when focus groups are under 45 minutes long. A 10-minute break is a must when focus groups last more than 45 minutes. This short recess is beneficial for the moderator, the comoderator, and the participants. The moderator and the comoderator can use this time to collect their thoughts and, if necessary, to modify plans for the remainder of the session. For example, they can determine (a) whether any of the issues raised by the participants need to be clarified or expanded, (b) whether they are progressing as planned, and (c) whether any changes need to be made in focus group procedures or seating. A break is also beneficial for participants. They can relax a bit from intense discussions and come back to the discussion with renewed energy. Also, given an opportunity to reflect, participants may thereafter spontaneously clarify or expand previously expressed ideas.

Cross-Reference Tip
To learn more about the responsibilities of the moderator and the comoderator during the focus group, please see Chapter 6, page 55 and Chapter 9, page 101.

Where Should Focus Groups Be Held?

Focus groups should be conducted in locations that participants can get to conveniently. Perhaps more important, the location must be a quiet, informal place that fosters openness and honesty in participants' remarks. The setting should promote interaction and discussion among the participants. Ideally, a neutral location will best accomplish these outcomes. That is, whenever possible, focus groups should be conducted in settings that will not be perceived by participants as the "territory" of an interested party. In practice though, availability or cost may make it necessary to consider settings that are not neutral. Therefore focus groups might be conducted in any of the following places:

- Neutral community settings
    Community centers
    Libraries
    Hotel conference rooms
    Churches
    Meeting rooms in public-service-oriented businesses (such as banks)

- Nonneutral school settings
  School buildings
  Administrative buildings or offices

Note that most of the locations suggested above are available at little or no cost. However, some locations such as hotel rooms tend to be quite expensive. Note also that a location considered "neutral" by most participants in most situations might in other situations not be considered neutral at all. For example, school prayer and public financing of services at private schools have been prominent issues in some communities. In these circumstances, a church location might well be seen as the territory of an interested party and therefore not considered a neutral location.

In any case, determining the importance of selecting a neutral over a nonneutral setting is dependent on the purpose of the focus group. That determination can be made judiciously by focusing on the following questions:

- Is the purpose of the focus group such that the participants will be required to make critical remarks about an institution (e.g., school or church policies, programs, services, or resources) or about the employees and members of that institution?
- If the nonneutral setting is used, will it interfere with the participants' ability to share information candidly?

If the answer to either of these two questions is "Yes," then a neutral setting must be used. Steve, for instance, should schedule focus groups in neutral locations. The possibility of a return to neighborhood schools could certainly elicit criticisms of the school system. A neutral location is also needed in Steve's case to ensure candid conversation about the "touchy" issues of previous discriminatory school policies.

However, if the answer to the foregoing two questions is "No," then a nonneutral setting may be used. If Steve does conduct another series of focus groups to identify ideas for developing a public information campaign, he might schedule the groups in the district administration building for reasons relating to convenience and cost. Given that the decision about neighborhood schools would already have been made, it is unlikely at this point that participants would need to critique district policies. Also, it is unlikely that the nonneutral setting would interfere with participants' candor.

After having considered the issue of neutral versus nonneutral locations, remember to also attend to the actual room in which the focus groups will be conducted. The room should be a quiet place in which a group can meet without any interruptions. For instance, the location of the room should be such that you will not be able to hear a lot of conversations or foot traffic. The room should not lead to any other room; in other words, it should not become a passage for others. Also, you should not have people coming into the room to pick up some material from the cabinets or to take a cup of coffee. Furthermore, the room should be free of other auditory and visual interruptions. For instance, if there is a PA system or telephone in the

FYI: Location of Focus Groups

Different opinions regarding the location of focus groups exist. However, none of these opinions have been empirically tested to determine if one is better than the other in making the focus groups participants more productive.

Some individuals who conduct focus groups believe that groups should be conducted only in neutral settings because the participants may be encumbered from expressing their opinions honestly in settings they are critically evaluating (Beck, Trombetta, & Share, 1986). For example, when the purpose of the focus group is to critically evaluate the school and its teachers, the participants of the focus group (parents, for example) may be more open and at ease in a nonschool neutral setting, such as a room in a library. However, Karger (1987) has made another suggestion. He suggests that focus groups be conducted in the participants' own real-life settings because other settings are, in effect, artificial environments that separate people from their normal behavior, thinking, and feelings. Still others believe that focus groups can be conducted in any setting as long as that location is quiet and relaxing and is conducive to participants interacting with each other and discussing their opinions honestly (Sevier, 1989; Wells, 1974).

Given the above range of opinions, we have addressed the issue of location by once again considering the purpose of the focus group.

room, you should be able to turn it off. As for visual interruptions, the room must be free of paintings, artwork, and displays that could be distracting to the participants. The goal here is to have the participants concentrate on the discussion and not be preoccupied with a painting or a display on a bulletin board. Finally, you should make sure that a table is available. Arranging chairs around a table is far better for focus group discussions than merely arranging the chairs in a circle without a table. The participants are more likely to feel relaxed and secure behind a table than they would out in the open.

How Many Focus Groups
Should Be Scheduled per Day?

The number of focus groups that can be scheduled per day for any project is limited by this firm guideline: only one focus group per day per moderator.

As you will learn in Chapter 9, the moderator's responsibilities during a focus group are challenging. The moderator must juggle tasks such as listening carefully to what is being said, watching for subtle body language of participants, remembering points of discussion that should later be clarified, and keeping track of the agenda. If your thought while reading the previous sentence was, "Wow, that makes me tired just thinking of doing that," you have perfectly understood the reason behind the guideline of one focus group per day per moderator. Doing a good job of moderating a focus group is tiring, and even an experienced moderator cannot be expected to be in top form for another focus group held the same day. Of course, more than one focus group can be scheduled per day if multiple moderators are being used in a focus group project. In other words, you could schedule two groups per day if you were using two moderators, three per day if you were using three moderators, and so on.

You now know how to go about making good decisions about scheduling the focus groups planned for your project. As we have explained, these decisions—at first, appearing to be relatively unimportant—are worth the time to consider carefully.

At a Glance:
Making Decisions About Scheduling Focus Groups

❏ Have I determined the size of the focus group?
❏ Have I determined how many focus groups are needed?
❏ Have I determined how many times each focus group will meet?
❏ Have I determined how long each focus group should last?
❏ Have I determined whether a break is needed during each focus group?
❏ Have I determined where each focus group is going to be held?
❏ Have I determined how many focus groups have to be scheduled per day?

6

Finalizing Important Details

Chapter at a Glance

- Should a comoderator be used?
- Are additional moderators needed to conduct the focus groups?
- Is an advance organizer needed?
- Should refreshments be provided?
- Should notes be taken?
- Should a tape recorder be used?
- Should participant consent be obtained?
- Should participants be remunerated?

You have already made a host of decisions, as discussed in the previous chapter, about scheduling focus groups. Now, you have just a few more matters to take care of before you reach the end of the decision-making process. The purpose of this chapter is to provide you with information that will help you make these decisions.

Should a Comoderator Be Used?

A comoderator is essentially a moderator's assistant. Any focus group, no matter how experienced the moderator, benefits by the presence of a comoderator. Therefore we encourage you to arrange for comoderating whenever possible for any focus group, and always in the case of a novice moderator. A moderator who has conducted a few focus groups or none at all will almost certainly need the extra pair of eyes, ears, and hands that a comoderator provides.

Typically, the moderator determines the responsibilities of the co-moderator. These responsibilities include assisting the moderator during the focus group as well as completing tasks before and after the discussion. If the absence of a comoderator is unavoidable, a moderator could also take on those responsibilities. However, a comoderator's responsibilities should not be taken lightly. Here are some of the ways in which a comoderator can be of assistance:

Cross-Reference Tip
To see an example depicting the role of a comoderator in a focus group, please see Chapter 8, page 88.

- Help set up the room
- Help greet the participants and make them comfortable before the focus group
- Handle the tape recorder (start and stop the machine as needed, turn the tape, and keep an eye on the machine to see whether it is recording)
- Complete the focus group monitoring checklist and inform the moderator when he or she has forgotten to do something during the focus group
- Take notes
- Assist the moderator with probing during discussion
- Monitor participants (for example, the moderator has not taken note of a participant who has been trying to say something—the comoderator notices and calls on the participant)

Are Additional Moderators Needed to Conduct the Focus Groups?

The task here is to determine whether the moderator you have selected can moderate all the focus groups to be held within your project or whether you will need to select additional moderators to conduct some of the groups. Although experts differ, we believe this decision can be made on the basis of the following three issues:

- Number of focus groups that are going to be conducted
- Amount of time the moderator has available
- Characteristics of the participants

If a small number of focus groups are being conducted and the moderator has sufficient work time available, he or she may be able to conduct all the focus groups without a second moderator to pick up some of the load.

However, if a large number of focus groups are being conducted, most likely it would be unworkable for one moderator to conduct all the groups. Even if that moderator were able to devote time to the project exclusively, the schedule would be exhausting and the quality of the information gathered might suffer. Conducting even one focus group consumes a great deal of mental energy, especially for a novice moderator. Moderators also cannot reasonably conduct several focus groups over a relatively short period of time. In these situations, it may be necessary to select another moderator.

The need for a second moderator is also determined by the characteristics of potential participants. As we discussed in Chapter 2, participants are more likely to respond openly when the moderator is seen as being similar to themselves in some ways. For that reason, you may need more than one moderator if you have more than one participant group. For example, if the purpose of your focus group project necessitates hearing from differing cultural groups, you should select additional moderators so each focus group will be moderated by a person of similar cultural background.

Another occasion in which you may need to select another moderator is when one of your participant groups includes children. Here, it is absolutely essential to have a moderator with whom children are at ease. Ideally, that moderator would also have experience in moderating focus groups with children.

> **Cross-Reference Tip**
> To learn more about selecting a moderator who has characteristics similar to those of the participants, please see Chapter 2, page 17.

Is an Advance Organizer Needed?

The task here is to decide whether an *advance organizer* is needed for the focus group project at hand. An advance organizer is brief, written information that is given to the focus group participants in advance of the focus group meeting. This information is intended to give participants a chance to "organize" their thoughts before they attend a focus group. An advance organizer could be designed in any of the following formats:

- A list of questions that will be asked during the focus group
- A list of questions to promote thinking on the focus group topic
- A statement explaining the purpose of the focus group
- An agenda of the focus group session

The decision to use an advance organizer depends on the purpose of the focus groups and also on your personal preference. The determination to use an advance organizer can be made judiciously by asking yourself the following questions:

- Given the purpose of the project, is prior exposure to the topic of discussion desired or required?

FYI: Should the Same Moderator Conduct All Focus Groups?

Should one moderator conduct all focus groups in a project? Sources disagree.

For instance, Karger (1987) notes,

> One facilitator must not be permitted to conduct all the study groups. Frequently observed phenomena are that a group leader stops listening after, say, three or four sessions on a given topic or gives greater subsequent interviewing attention to the most striking insights derived from prior sessions. This is a prescription for using different facilitators for a study. (p. 54)

On the contrary, Bellenger, Bernhardt, and Goldstucker (1976) note,

> It is important to use the same moderator for all the group sessions. . . . The moderator learns from each session, and becomes more effective in subsequent sessions. He is actually fine tuning his final report with each additional group. (p. 20)

Given our emphasis on practicality and the lack of research data, our opinion is that one or more moderators could be used, based on practical and logistical concerns. Regardless of the number, adhering to the following safeguards is important:

- Schedule no more than one focus group per day per moderator.
- Ensure that moderators approach each group with no preconceived notions.
- Use a checklist for moderating the focus groups.
- Have a post-focus-group meeting after each focus group.
- Arrange for a comoderator whenever possible.

- Would exposure to the topic ahead of time benefit the focus group discussion?
- Given the purpose of the project, would prior exposure to the topic of discussion be undesirable or unwarranted?
- Would exposure to the topic ahead of time compromise the trustworthiness, integrity, and quality of the information collected?

For instance, consider Mike, who is a teacher and a team leader at a middle school. Mike is developing a short consumer satisfaction survey to obtain parental feedback on the parent-teacher conferences to be held the following week. He wants quick feedback from other teachers to determine whether he is headed in the right direction as he drafts the survey. He

Advance Organizer

Home-School Communication

During the focus group, we will be talking about the following subjects:

- The problems you are facing or have faced in communicating with the teachers at your child's school
- Your expectations of the teachers regarding their communication with you

conducts a brief impromptu focus group with a group of teachers after school. In this case, an advance organizer is not only unnecessary but also impractical.

Also consider Carol, who wants to conduct focus groups with students to determine why an after-school homework lab is not being used by the students. She wants to know about the limitations of the homework lab, other reasons for not using the lab, and ways the lab could be improved. Because there are several aspects to her purpose, she may want to use an advance organizer so the students have an opportunity to collect their thoughts.

Finally, consider John, a high school principal who wants to conduct focus groups to determine how students feel about school uniforms. John may decide not to use the advance organizer: He does not want to take the chance that the opinions and feelings of students participating in the focus groups will be influenced beforehand by the views of other students.

When participants are given an advance organizer, they will have an opportunity to think about the topic ahead of time and may also discuss the topic with others. Consequently, they may share ideas at the focus group meeting that they may not have originated. If this is not what you want to happen, then do not use an advance organizer.

Should Refreshments Be Provided?

It is customary to provide some light refreshments for the participants during a focus group (e.g., soft drinks, coffee, tea, cookies, or fruit and cheese). In fact, refreshments become almost a necessity when focus groups are of long duration (i.e., 1 to 1½ hours or more). Refreshments are essential for establishing a comfortable atmosphere before and during a focus group. Participants will be more inclined to relax and unwind as they wait for the focus group to begin and will again be refreshed during the break. Just as important, a refreshment table will facilitate interaction and communication among the participants.

Should Notes Be Taken?

It is a good idea to take notes during a focus group discussion. Of course, one advantage of note taking is that you will have a written record of what the participants are saying. But just as important is that you will have a record of the messages conveyed by participants' body language (e.g., facial expressions showing difference of opinion or heads nodding in agreement). On the downside, it would be extremely difficult for the moderator to take such comprehensive notes during a focus group. The moderator cannot do a good job of moderating the discussion if he or she has to simultaneously listen to the participants, think of the probes needed to be asked, guide the discussion, and take notes. In fact, it is next to impossible to take comprehensive notes and also moderate the discussion effectively.

Thus your first task here is to determine whether you need comprehensive notes. This can be done by thinking ahead about the method you will use to analyze the focus group information (see Chapter 10 for an in-depth explanation of the various methods for analyzing focus group information). If the method you choose to analyze focus group information requires comprehensive, dependable notes, it is essential to assign the task of note taking to an individual other than the moderator. A comoderator could be held responsible for this task. But, before assigning this responsibility, you need to consider the feasibility of such an assignment given the comoderator's other responsibilities. Another option would be to have a note taker whose sole responsibility is to take notes. On the other hand, if comprehensive notes are not desired, another option would be to note only the main points of the discussion and all relevant nonverbal behaviors. Such a decision would limit the amount of notes that have to be taken by the moderator or the comoderator and would make the task of note taking more manageable.

Should a Tape Recorder Be Used?

Yes, you should use a tape recorder to audiotape the focus group discussions. Tape-recording has certain advantages. One of the main advantages is that there will be a permanent record of the focus group discussion. Another advantage is that it is not necessary to take comprehensive notes during the discussion unless it has been decided that comprehensive notes

Recording Equipment: Some Tips

1. If you have some recording equipment, test its quality in a group situation or in a mock focus group. If the equipment is working fine but the recording is not clear, you will need a better microphone. Using the built-in microphone on a tape recorder is not recommended because it is not sensitive enough.
2. You can use any tape recorder, but if you are looking for a professional quality tape recorder with two tape decks, check out some audio stores listed in the Yellow Pages.
3. Use a good-quality microphone to get an excellent recording. We recommend using a "boundary" microphone. It is also referred to as a pressure-sensitive microphone. It is flat and when kept on the table, it is unobtrusive. It also picks up less background noise than an omnidirectional microphone. The cost of this microphone is around $40 to $50. You can buy it from any audio store, including RadioShack.

are necessary for analyzing the focus group information. Even if notes are taken, one can use the audiotapes at a later time to augment the details in the notes. Furthermore, in the presence of a tape recorder, participants may feel that their contributions are important and are therefore being heeded. However, to realize these advantages, it is essential to use quality equipment: The recorded audiotapes will be useful only if the recordings are clear and intelligible.

Despite these important advantages, tape-recording may also have some limitations. A tape recorder registers only the verbalizations of the participants and does not provide any information communicated by means of body language (e.g., frowns, nods, anger, or frustration). Also, some of the participants' comments may be lost when a tape is being turned over. Finally, some participants may not be comfortable and candid in the presence of a tape recorder, and some may decide not to participate at all. To offset these possible disadvantages, participants must be made aware in advance of the audiotaping and the manner in which the tapes will be used (e.g., destroyed after use). Also, during the recruitment process, the guarantees and assurances listed in the participant consent form (described in the next section) must be clearly communicated to the participants. Furthermore, moderators and comoderators should be available to the participants by phone in the days preceding the focus group session to alleviate any concerns and reservations the participants might have. Finally, the recording equipment must be placed unobtrusively during the focus group.

Cross-Reference Tips

To learn about what a moderator can say to prevent participants from talking over each other so the recordings are clear, please see Chapter 8, page 88.

To learn about the mechanics of analyzing focus group information using audiotapes, please see Chapter 10, page 119.

Form 6.1. Participant Consent Form

I, _____, agree to participate in the focus group conducted by Ray West and Joyce Green for the Elm Park School District.

I understand that . . .

The purpose of the focus group is to determine how I feel about the proposed bond issue.

What I say will be used in developing a public awareness campaign and in determining whether the bond issue should be placed on the ballot.

A value judgment will not be made about me based on my comments.

My name will not be mentioned in summary reports or anywhere else.

I have the opportunity to remove my comments from the summary reports at any time.

I will not discuss other participants' comments outside this group.

The discussion will be audiotaped and then transcribed.

The audiotapes will be destroyed after the transcription.

Signature _____ Date _____

Should Participant Consent Be Obtained?

It is customary to obtain consent from participants in writing before they participate in a focus group. The goals of obtaining consent are to ensure that participants are well informed about the focus group and that there are no hidden surprises for them. For their consent to actually be *informed consent*, participants need to understand the purpose of the focus group and how the resulting information will be used. They also need to know how the audiotapes will be used and how the confidentiality of their comments will be protected. See Form 6.1 for a sample participant consent form addressing these and other assurances and guarantees.

Obtaining consent from the participants is essential to establishing an atmosphere of trust and comfort that we hope will pave the way for complete and candid disclosure during the focus group. Consent can be obtained in writing from the participants on the day of the focus group. But if the participants are children, written consent should be obtained from their parents or guardians prior to scheduling them for the group. See Form 6.2 for a sample parent/guardian consent form. If the children are old enough to understand the assurances and guarantees listed in the consent form, the consent form could also be shared with them.

Form 6.2. Parent/Guardian Consent Form

I, _____, agree to allow _____ to participate
in the focus group conducted by Ray West and Joyce Green for the Elm Park
Middle School.

I understand that . . .

The purpose of the focus group is to determine how students feel about the new
interactive math program.
What my son/daughter says will be used toward making a
decision regarding the effectiveness of the new curriculum.
A value judgment will not be made about my son/daughter based on his/her
comments.
My son's/daughter's name will not be mentioned in summary reports or anywhere
else.
I have the opportunity to remove my son's/daughter's comments from the summary
reports at any time.
The discussion will be audiotaped.
The audiotapes will be destroyed after detailed notes have been taken.

Signature _____ Date _____

Should Participants Be Remunerated?

Depending on the availability of resources, participants may be remunerated for their time and effort. Sometimes, remuneration is essential for facil-
itating and ensuring the participation of those who are difficult to reach or
unwilling to participate. A typical remuneration is around $20 to $25. In
some cases, remuneration is merely a gesture of appreciation and goodwill
and could go as low as $15. Even then, be warned that unless you use the
minimum wage as a guideline, you may not actually generate much goodwill. When participants are difficult to schedule, such as groups of administrators or business leaders, remuneration may go as high as $100.

However, before using monetary compensations as incentives to encourage participation of any group, consider whether money will actually
make a difference in people's decisions to participate in a focus group. If
not, using monetary incentives would be an unwise use of resources. Consider alternatives to money. Ask yourself, "Is there another incentive that
will really help the participants?" For example, provision of child care is
sometimes a better incentive than money. When parents consider participation in a focus group, they may be wondering, "So, who will take care of my
children? Where can I leave them?" In such cases, provision of child care

might increase participation more than money would. Participants would be able to attend the focus groups while their children were being looked after in the next room.

In this chapter, we have described more issues that you need to think about before recruiting participants and conducting focus groups. Although some of the topics mentioned in this chapter seem like common sense, please note, they are still areas that need to be attended. Another area that needs to be resolved is determining whether additional moderators are needed. Remember, you cannot make this decision until you have determined the composition of the focus groups and the logistics for conducting them.

At a Glance: Finalizing Important Details

❏ Have I determined who the comoderator will be?
❏ Have I determined whether I need an additional moderator?
  ❏ If "Yes," have I identified the person?
❏ Have I determined whether an advance organizer is needed?
  ❏ If "Yes," have I developed it?
❏ Have I determined whether refreshments are needed?
  ❏ If "Yes," have I determined what refreshments to serve?
❏ Have I determined the need for taking notes?
  ❏ If "Yes," have I identified the person for the job?
❏ Am I ready with my recording equipment?
❏ Have I developed the participant consent form?
❏ Have I determined whether the participants are to be remunerated?
  ❏ If "Yes," have I determined the nature of the remunerations?

7

Recruiting Participants

Chapter at a Glance

- What are the sources for recruiting participants?
- Which participants should be contacted from the sources?
- How can participants be contacted?
- How are participants screened?
- How should participants be selected?
- What does the task of scheduling participants involve?

If you are scheduling a focus group to be composed of teachers from your school, the process of recruiting participants could be as simple as making a few telephone calls. More often, however, recruiting conjures up images of endless phone calls, unwilling participants, scheduling nightmares, and finally, no-shows. This unpleasant scenario can be avoided, even for large focus group projects. By knowing how to carry out the recruiting process in a professional and organized manner, you will be able to keep the recruiting tasks from getting overly complicated and the recruiters from getting demoralized. The purpose of this chapter is to delineate the recruiting process in a step-by-step manner. You will then have a complete picture of everything that needs to be done both before and after contacting the participants, all the decisions to be made, and all the tasks that have to be completed.

What Are the Sources for Recruiting Participants?

The recruitment process starts with the task of determining sources for recruiting participants. In other words, where can you find participants? Focus group participants can be recruited in two ways:

- From existing lists and databases
- By referrals

Existing lists and databases such as the following could be used as sources to screen and select participants:

- School database
- School district database
- Local telephone directory

For most school-based focus group projects, it may be sufficient to recruit participants from the school database or from the school district database. But for certain focus group projects, you may need to tap into several databases to recruit participants. For instance, suppose a large urban school district has had yet another superintendent resign. The school board wants to maximize the chances that the hiring process will locate a superintendent who can garner the widespread support necessary to stabilize district operations. Therefore school board members might make extensive use of several existing databases: families and high school students from the school district database, teachers from the teachers' union database, and business representatives from the chamber of commerce database.

Good sources for referrals are often people who participated in previous focus group projects or who did not meet the selection criteria for the current project. Of course, any individual could be a source for referrals that lead to additional participants. For example, imagine that an assistant superintendent is exploring the idea of an "Adopt-a-School" program in her district. She decides to conduct some focus groups with community business leaders to understand how to enlist the help of as many businesses as possible. She calls the business leaders she happens to know and asks them for the names of other business leaders who might be interested.

Which Participants Should Be Contacted From the Sources?

The task here is to decide whether all the potential participants from the list and/or database will be contacted or whether only a certain number of them will be contacted. If the decision is the latter, then obviously you need to choose some names from among others. So, how does one begin? Which persons should you choose to contact? Which name do you start with first? You will need to somehow reduce a long list to a smaller, more manageable list of potential participants. Rather than going about this haphazardly, here are some suggestions for identifying participants in a systematic and sound manner:

- You can choose every "nth" person from a list, with "n" being any ordinal number (i.e., 1st, 2nd, 3rd, and so on). For example, if you decide to choose every 10th person, you would choose the 10th person from the beginning of the list and every 10th person thereafter until you reach the end of the list. If you do not have a sufficient number of participants when you have reached the end of the list, you can choose another ordinal number and repeat the process.
- When using lists that are arranged in an alphabetical order, you can begin with the names starting with the letter A. Choose two, three, five, or any other number of participants. Then, move on to the names starting with B and choose the same number of participants.
- You can divide the number on the list by the number of potential participants needed and use that number to select. For example, if you need 100 names from a list of 1,000 people, you would select every 10th person.

How Can Participants Be Contacted?

After identifying potential partcipants, the next step in the recruitment process is to contact them. However, there are really two tasks at this point: first determining how contact will be made and then actually contacting participants. In this section, we explain these two tasks.

Determining the Method for Contacting Participants. The task here is to decide how the potential participants are going to be contacted. There are several ways of contacting the participants: telephone call, face-to-face, letter by mail or e-mail, or letter sent home with students. Selecting one of these is guided by two factors: (1) the source for contacting participants and (2) the advantages and disadvantages of each of these methods.

When the source is the school database, participants can be contacted in any manner. On the other hand, when the source is a telephone directory, telephone calls would be the most practical option. Usually, though, the decision is not so linear: You must consider the advantages and the disadvantages shown in Table 7.1 before making a decision. For instance, contacting participants by mail may make the focus group project look more credible to the potential participants; however, it is time-consuming and effort-intensive. Contacting participants by phone, on the other hand, is relatively efficient. Nonetheless, potential participants may make on-the-spot decisions, deciding not to participate in the project on the basis of their first impressions of the caller. Additional advantages and disadvantages of each method (telephone call, face-to-face, or letter by mail, e-mail, or via students) are discussed in Table 7.1.

Sometimes, decisions regarding the method for contacting the participants are also guided by the prevailing conditions at the school. For example, consider a school that has a working communication system between home and school and enjoys a high degree of parental involvement. In this case, a letter sent home via the students' weekly communication folders is a viable option. Now, consider a school with a relatively uninvolved parent population. This school has found that sending letters home with the students does not usually get results. Because many parents do not have a telephone in their homes, telephone contact is not a viable option either. Obviously, contacting participants in such a situation would be a challenge, and more than one method of contacting participants would have to be employed.

Contacting the Participants. After determining the method for contacting the participants, the next step is to contact them. If the participants are going to be contacted by mail, e-mail, or by sending information home with students, a letter needs to be composed, and a participant sign-up form needs to be developed. The letter should be short and to the point and no more than one page in length. However, you should take care to include certain minimum information so the participants can make informed decisions. The following questions can be used as a starting point in composing letters that meet the minimum requirements for being informative:

> **Cross-Reference Tip**
> To learn more about tape-recording, confidentiality of participants' comments, and remunerating participants, please see Chapter 6, pages 60-64.

- Who are you (the person contacting the participant)?
- How did you get the name of the participant?
- What is the reason for contacting the participant?
- What is required of the participants?
- How can the participants help you?
- What is a focus group?
- When will the focus group be held?
- How long will the focus group last?
- What is the remuneration?
- Will participant remarks be kept confidential?
- Will the discussion be tape-recorded?

Of course, there will be instances when it is not necessary to cover all the above information in a letter. For instance, if a letter is being sent from the administrative office to the teachers in the school district, it is not necessary to clarify who the writer is or how the teachers' names were obtained. Simi-

Table 7.1   Advantages and Disadvantages of Different Methods of Contacting Participants

Type of Contact	Advantages	Disadvantages
Telephone call	• Participant response time is less than when participants are contacted by mail. • During one call, it is possible to inform the participant, gather information from the participant, and determine if the participant will qualify. • Calls are efficient when screening criteria are not stringent. Participants will qualify easily and fewer calls will have to be made.	• Thanks to telemarketing, potential participants may not be willing to talk to you or may brush you off. • There may be difficulty in contacting the participant due to caller ID, voice mail, and so on. • First impressions do matter. Participants may make on-the-spot decisions, and the chances of losing a participant may be high.
Face-to-face	• This is an easy way to contact participants, especially within a setting such as at staff meetings, open houses.	• This method is impractical when contacting participants requires you to travel to a number of places.
Letter by mail	• A mail contact may look more "official" and may therefore seem more important and credible than a telephone contact.	• Participant response time is more than when participants are contacted by telephone. • Mailing is expensive and effort-intensive when a large number of people have to be contacted. • Follow-up mailings or telephone calls may be necessary when potential participants do not respond.
Letter by e-mail	• A quick, efficient way of contacting people. • The computer creates a record of exactly when the contact was made, especially if you include a request for a receipt in your e-mail server settings.	• Some parents may not be accessible by e-mail due to lack of computers at home or at work. • E-mail may not appeal to some because they may consider it too informal; it may be viewed as being more suitable for follow-up contact rather than initial contact.
Letter sent home with students	• This is less expensive and effort-intensive than mailing.	• Students may lose the letter. • Letters may get overlooked in the paper trail that comes from school. • A follow-up telephone call or another letter sent home may be necessary.

larly, the letter will include information on remuneration only if the participants are being compensated in some manner.

In addition to the letter itself, a *participant sign-up form* (see Form 7.1) needs to be developed. Its purpose is to organize all the information that is to be collected from the participants during the recruitment process. The participant sign-up form includes items from the following areas:

- Relevant participant characteristics (for example, name and gender)
- Participant contact information (for example, additional phone numbers and best times to contact)
- Scheduling issues (for example, the days and times that would be most convenient for them to attend a focus group)
- Previously identified screening criteria (see the following example)

Cross-Reference Tip
During the recruitment process, participants are screened according to the screening criteria identified in Chapter 4. To learn about the screening criteria, please see Chapter 4, page 33.

Now, consider the following example. A high school was offering an innovative math curriculum in place of the traditional one. However, many parents and students had expressed their dissatisfaction with this new program. Sarah, the assistant principal in charge of curriculum, wanted to conduct two focus groups with parents and another two with students to learn more about their concerns. (See her recruiting letter on page 71.) The screening criteria she identified as being relevant to the parent focus groups included the following:

- Purpose-based criteria: participants' dissatisfaction with the program
- Demographic criteria: gender of the participants
- Exclusion criteria: prior focus group participation, expert or authority figure

If the participants are going to be contacted by telephone or face to face, a *screening questionnaire* needs to be developed so the recruiter can record in writing the information the participants give them verbally. A screening questionnaire includes all the elements of a letter and the participant sign-up form. It is designed to inform the participants, gather information from them, and at the same time help you make decisions about qualifying the participants for the focus group project. A sample screening questionnaire is presented in Form 7.2.

Screening questionnaires are usually in the form of a script specifying what to say to the participants and when to say it. The structure and order imposed by the questionnaires help you guarantee that all potential participants are being contacted in the same manner and all the required minimum information is being conveyed to each one. Consequently, potential participants will be able to make well-informed decisions. Also, they will not encounter any hidden surprises at a later stage, such as "Oh! I was not told that the session is being tape-recorded." The need for this structure and order is underscored when multiple individuals are involved in the recruiting process.

Contacting potential participants via telephone or face to face requires special care. First impressions do matter: You can gain or lose a potential participant on the basis of what you say and how you say it. It is therefore essential that you actually rehearse the screening questionnaire and not just be familiar with it. By rehearsing, you will be able to communicate the required information clearly and succinctly, in the shortest period of time, and also in a congenial manner.

Here is a cautionary note about contacting students: If the participants for the focus groups are students, parental consent needs to be obtained prior to contacting the students themselves. Therefore parents will have to be contacted first and their consent obtained in writing. Only then can you contact the students to ask them whether they would be interested in participating in the focus groups.

Cross-Reference Tip
To see a sample parent consent form, please see Chapter 6, page 63.

Sample Letter

November 28, 2001

Dear Mr. & Ms. Wright,

We are aware that some parents have been dissatisfied with the new math curriculum that is being offered at the school. We will therefore be conducting a focus group project at Snyder High School to discuss these parent concerns. The information gathered from the focus group will help the math department in determining the future course of action.

The focus group will take less than 2 hours of your time and will be conducted in January. It will be conducted at a time that is convenient to you and all the other participants. We will have about six to eight participants; they will sit around a table and discuss the math curriculum. There will be a moderator to guide the discussion, and the focus group discussion will be tape-recorded. After detailed notes have been taken, the tapes will be destroyed. Anything you say at the focus group will be kept confidential, and your name will not be mentioned outside the focus group or in any report.

Here is an opportunity for you to tell us how you feel. Please note, though, only one of you can participate in the focus group. Let us know which one of you will be representing your family at the focus group.

Please complete and return the enclosed participant sign-up form by December 11th, 2001. We will then contact you by phone to set up a date and time for the focus group discussion.

We would like to hear from you. We hope you will consider participating in the focus group discussion.

Sincerely,

Ms. Sarah West

Assistant Principal

Form 7.1. Sample Participant Sign-up Form

Parent

Name of Parent/Guardian _____ Gender _____

Address _____

Phone (home) _____ Best time to reach you _____

Phone (work) _____ Can we contact you at work? _____

E-mail _____

Participant's occupation _____

Preferred days to participate in the focus group _____

Preferred times to participate in the focus group _____

How do you feel about the new math curriculum? (Check one.)

____ Satisfied
____ Somewhat satisfied
____ Somewhat dissatisfied
____ Dissatisfied

How would you rate your knowledge of the new math program?

____ Very knowledgeable
____ Knowledgeable
____ Somewhat knowledgeable
____ Not at all knowledgeable

Have you participated in a focus group before? (Circle one.)

Yes   No

If yes, was it within the last 2 years? (Circle one.)

Yes   No

If yes, how many? _____

Form 7.2.   Sample Screening Questionnaire

Hello _____ (Ms./Mrs./Mr. last name). My name is _____ (full name). I am calling you on behalf of Ms. West, the assistant principal at Snyder High School. I got your name from the school database. I am calling to tell you about the focus group project that is going to be conducted at Snyder High School. The topic of discussion for the focus group will be the new math curriculum. I need about 5 minutes of your time to explain more about the project and tell you why I am calling you. May I continue, or should I call back at a better time? *[If later, ask when you can call back. Get a time, thank the person, and hang up.]*

We are aware that some parents have been dissatisfied with the new math curriculum, and we want to hear from them. Here is an opportunity for the parents to tell us how they feel. The purpose of the focus group project is to discuss parents' concerns and reservations regarding this new math curriculum. The information gathered from the focus group will help Ms. West and the math department in determining the future course of action. I would like to ask you some questions to see if you would qualify for our project.

Have you participated in a focus group before? (Circle one.)   Yes   No
If "Yes," was it within the last 2 years? (Circle one.)   Yes   No   How many? ____
[Terminate if number is four groups or more. For this and all other occasions when a person does not qualify for participation, briefly explain why, answer any questions, thank the person, and then hang up.]

How would you rate your knowledge of the new math curriculum?

____ Very knowledgeable   ____ Somewhat knowledgeable
____ Knowledgeable   ____ Not at all knowledgeable
[Terminate if "Very knowledgeable" or "Knowledgeable."]

How do you feel about the new math curriculum? (Check one.)
____ Satisfied   ____ Somewhat dissatisfied
____ Somewhat satisfied   ____ Dissatisfied
[Terminate if "Satisfied" or "Somewhat satisfied."]

We could definitely use you as a participant in our project. In fact, we would like to hear your views. Let me tell you a little bit more about the focus group itself. The focus group will take less than 2 hours of your time and will be conducted in the month of January. The group will be conducted at a time that is convenient to you and all the other participants. We will have about six to eight participants in the focus group; they will sit around a table and discuss the math curriculum. There will be a moderator to guide the discussion, and the focus group discussion will be tape-recorded. After detailed notes are taken, the tapes will be destroyed. Anything you say at the focus group will be kept confidential. Your name will not be mentioned outside the focus group or in any report. Can we count on you as someone interested in participating in the focus group?   Yes   No
[Terminate if "No."]

If "Yes," thank you. I need to get some more information from you.

Name of Parent/Guardian _____ Gender _____
Address _____
_____
Phone (home) _____ Best time to reach you _____
Phone (work) _____ Can we contact you at work? _____
E-mail _____
Participant's occupation _____
Preferred days to participate in the focus group _____
Preferred times to participate in the focus group _____

We will call you back to schedule a focus group. Thank you.

How Are Participants Screened?

Screening participants essentially involves qualifying them according to predetermined criteria. Remember, when participants are contacted by telephone or face-to-face, the task of qualifying them is accomplished during the contact itself. However, when participants are contacted by letter (mailed, e-mailed, or carried home by students), you do not carry out the task of qualifying the participants until interested individuals have returned the completed sign-up forms. To better understand the mechanics of the screening process, reflect once again on the participant sign-up form (Form 7.1) used by Sarah. On the basis of the completed forms, Sarah first made a pool of all the parents who were dissatisfied with the math program. From this pool, she excluded two parents because they had participated in six focus groups conducted by marketing firms over the last year and a half. Then, Sarah excluded one participant who was a judge. She believed this participant would represent an authority figure to the rest of the potential participants. None of the potential participants perceived themselves to be very knowledgeable about the math program so she did not exclude any of them on the basis of their expert status. Finally, Sarah had a pool of participants who were willing to take part in the focus group project and who met all the screening criteria. Note that although participant gender was a demographic screening criterion for her project, Sarah had both men and women in the participant pool. She would use the screening criterion of gender later, when scheduling the participants for each focus group. She had decided *not* to include both men and women in any one focus group because she believed she would get better information from same-gender groups.

How Should Participants Be Selected?

Sometimes, the pool of potential participants who have agreed to participate in the focus groups and who have met the screening criteria is small. In such instances, most, if not all, potential participants will be used for the focus groups; therefore the question of selecting some of them is a moot issue. However, at other times, the pool of potential participants is large enough that all the participants cannot be used for the focus group project. In such cases, it is necessary to select the required number of participants from the large pool systematically or randomly. Systematic or random selection of participants will prevent unnecessary biases from entering the selection process. Systematic selection involves selecting, for example, every second, or every fifth participant from the list. Random selection of participants can be achieved in many different ways. However, it is beyond the scope of this book to explain the more sophisticated of these strategies. One simple way of randomly selecting participants involves picking names out of a jar until you have a sufficient number of potential participants.

What Does the Task of Scheduling Participants Involve?

We have already discussed the first of the two main objectives for the participant recruitment process: to get the participants to agree to participate in the focus group. Now, we address the other equally important objective: to get them to attend. The key to achieving the second objective is to schedule focus groups at a time when the participants can indeed attend. However, this is easier said than done. Sometimes, finding the time when all six to eight participants can meet is a definite challenge.

After having scheduled the participants, it is advisable to send a confirmation letter. This letter should include the following information:

- Purpose of the focus group project
- Date, day, and time of the focus group
- Duration of the focus group
- Details about remuneration (if applicable)
- Confidentiality of participant comments and other pertinent assurances and guarantees
- Dress (e.g., casual clothes will suffice)
- Importance of being on time

If an advance organizer is used, remember to send it along with the confirmation letter. If it is not possible to send a confirmation letter, you would be wise to convey the information via a telephone call or e-mail. If resources permit, calling and reminding participants a day or two in advance of the focus group will be a great help in reducing no-shows.

Cross-Reference Tip
To learn about an advance organizer, please see Chapter 6, page 57.

As you have seen in this chapter, recruiting participants involves many details. Careful attention to these details will ensure that you locate the people whose views are needed for the particular purpose of your project. Also, by attending to the recruitment procedures outlined in this chapter, you will know you have done what is needed to ensure that enough potential participants agree to participate and that they will actually attend the focus group.

At a Glance: Recruiting Participants

❏ Have I determined the source for recruiting participants?
❏ Have I identified the potential participants I wish to contact?
❏ Have I determined the method for contacting the participants?

If contacting by mail, e-mail, or via students:
❏ Have I written the letter and developed the participant sign-up form?
❏ Have I mailed or e-mailed the information or sent the information home via students?

If contacting by telephone or face to face:
❏ Have I developed the screening questionnaire?
❏ Have I (and/or other recruiters) rehearsed the screening questionnaire?
❏ Have I screened the participants?
❏ Have I determined whether the participants need to be systematically or randomly selected?
❏ Have I scheduled the participants?
❏ Have I sent them a confirmation letter?
❏ Have I made a decision about reminder calls?

8

Developing a
Focus Group Guide

Chapter at a Glance

- What is a focus group guide?
- What items are needed to conduct a focus group?
- How should the room be set up?
- What should be done as the participants arrive?
- What should be said at the beginning of the focus group?
- What are the main questions?
- What are the areas for probing?
- How can a focus group discussion be monitored?
- How are focus group guides tested?

Poor Planning

Bill was the principal of an inner-city elementary school. There was a lot of mistrust and ill feeling between the parents and the teachers. Consequently, the morale at this school was very poor. So, Bill decided to conduct focus groups to identify the problem areas and to generate some ideas for resolving this problem. His initial plan was for three parent focus groups and three teacher focus groups, with a back-up plan to conduct more groups as necessary. He gave some thought to how he was going to conduct the focus groups; for example, he requested a teacher's aide to function as a comoderator. However, he did not develop a comprehensive plan by putting his ideas and thoughts down on paper in an organized manner. That is, he failed to develop a focus group guide.

Like a principal of any school, Bill was extremely busy at the time. To complicate matters, several weeks went by before he was able to carry out his initial plan and to actually conduct the first focus group. Consequently, many things did not go as he intended. For instance, he forgot to explain the ground rules for the discussion, which resulted in unpleasant dynamics among a few of the participants. Furthermore, because participants kept talking over each other, their remarks were not clear on the recorded tape (which was to be a back-up for the hand notes). There was also some confusion as to what the comoderator was supposed to do. For example, one area of confusion was about note taking. Neither Bill nor the aide took notes during the first focus group because each assumed that the other one was responsible. Another area of confusion was about the tape recorder. During one focus group, neither leader checked to make sure it was recording properly. Due to these and other missteps, Bill was unhappy with the final result. He believed that the product was not worth the time he had invested. Unfortunately, it was only in retrospect that Bill realized the importance of organizing his thoughts and ideas and putting them down on paper.

Better Planning

June was an active member of a PTA at an elementary school that boasted of a high degree of parental involvement. Although the status quo at the school did seem satisfactory, June sincerely believed there was always room for growth. So, she decided to conduct three focus groups with parents, scheduled in the evenings, to identify areas for further improvement. June also elicited the help of two other PTA parents, Mary as the comoderator and Lisa as the note taker. Furthermore, June spent some time developing a focus group guide. Because of this careful planning, June's focus groups were conducted consistently and efficiently. More important, the focus groups were productive, providing the information June had set out to obtain.

This chapter on developing a focus group guide will help you ensure that your focus group project goes as smoothly as June's did, without the disappointments of Bill's project. Although Bill did give some thought to how he was going to conduct the focus group, he did not take sufficient time, the way June did, to develop a focus group guide that spelled out every task for conducting it. In this chapter, guidelines for developing a focus group guide are delineated and these guidelines are illustrated by details from June's focus group guide.

What Is a Focus Group Guide?

A focus group guide is a protocol that stipulates in writing the questions to be asked of the participants. But it goes far beyond details about the topic to be discussed. The guide must detail everything that needs to be said and done. It begins with setting up the room before the participants arrive and ends with gathering up materials and equipment after the focus group is finished and all participants have left. Therefore all sorts of details will be specified, including how the participants will be greeted as they arrive, the parameters and ground rules for the discussion, and the roles for all involved—moderator, comoderator, and participants.

A focus group guide is extremely important from two perspectives: procedural efficiency and procedural consistency. As for procedural efficiency, a focus group guide is very useful because it helps a moderator conduct a well-planned and smoothly run focus group. The time that moderators and participants have devoted to the focus group will be well spent. Also, because the details have been taken care of, the moderator and the participants can direct their attention to the real matter at hand, the topic of discussion.

The focus group guide is also important with respect to procedural consistency. By procedural consistency, we mean making sure the same message is being conveyed, the same questions are being asked, and the same tasks are being performed in the same sequence across all focus groups in a given project. Without this assurance, you cannot be certain that any differences in ideas expressed across focus groups were real differences in participants' opinions and not the result of differences in the way the focus groups were conducted. Without procedural consistency, you cannot have confidence in the information you gathered. Just as important, others receiving the information may not view it as trustworthy. The need for procedural consistency is especially critical when the same moderator will not conduct all the focus groups in a project or when a comoderator is not a part of the focus group to "keep an eye" on things.

A focus group guide has seven parts:

1. Materials: What items are needed for a focus group?
2. Room setup: What should be done to set up the room?
3. Participant arrival: What should be done as the participants arrive?
4. Beginning the group: What should be said at the beginning of the focus group?
5. Main questions: What are the main questions?
6. Probing areas: What are the areas for probing?
7. Monitoring focus groups: How can focus groups be monitored?

In the ensuing sections, we explain each of these seven parts.

What Items Are Needed to Conduct a Focus Group?

For this task, you can begin by asking, "Considering the location and the room in which the focus group will be held, what are all the items that will be needed for conducting the focus group?" Your answer should be in the form of a written list. By using this list, time will not be wasted with last-minute trips to retrieve forgotten items. For instance, one frequently overlooked item is the extension cord needed to connect and appropriately place the tape recorder and the microphone. Another common oversight is delivering remuneration. If participants are going to be remunerated, it is essential to determine beforehand how they are going to be remunerated (e.g., cash or check) and to prepare the remuneration envelopes ahead of time. In general, your focus groups will run smoothly from beginning to end if you have made sure that everything that is needed is there. June, the PTA member, decided what she would need for her focus group and developed the list shown in the box on page 81.

How Should the Room Be Set Up?

Cross-Reference Tip
To learn about selecting a room for conducting a focus group, please see Chapter 5, page 51.

Identifying in advance all the tasks that should be done to set up a room serves a very important purpose. It helps in defining the division of responsibilities between the moderator and the comoderator. This in turn helps avoid last-minute confusion and misunderstandings. Therefore when setting up the room, consider the following tasks:

- Remove visual distractions (e.g., paintings, posters, bulletin boards, or displays of student artwork).
- Turn off auditory distractions (e.g., PA system or telephone).
- Connect and test recording equipment. Remember to keep the tape recorder in an unobtrusive place.
- Lay out the refreshments.
- Arrange other required material (e.g., pens or agendas).

June, the PTA member, also made a list of all the tasks that had to be completed to set up the room. She then divided the tasks between Mary (the comoderator) and herself (the moderator). June's list is presented in the box on page 82.

June's List of Focus Group Items

- 10 participant consent forms
- 10 name tags
- Markers for filling out name tags
- Pens for completing consent forms
- 3 clipboards
- 3 notepads
- Tape recorder and microphone
- Extension cords
- 90-minute tapes (label the tapes)
- New batteries
- Cookies (2 dozen) and cookie tray
- Cold drinks—cans (diet and regular)
- Cooler and ice
- Thermos of coffee
- Powdered cream
- Coffee stirrers
- Sugar and sugar substitute
- Napkins
- Small paper plates and cups

What Should Be Done as the Participants Arrive?

Here, you will note all the tasks that need to be completed from the time the first participant arrives until the beginning of the focus group itself. The main tasks here are to greet the participants, let them know the agenda, and make them feel comfortable. During this time, participants are requested to put on the name tags and complete the consent forms. Because the goal is to make the participants comfortable, it is important to explain the assurances and guarantees mentioned in the consent form and to answer any questions. Participants are also made aware of the refreshments and told to help themselves.

Cross-Reference Tip
To learn more about the participant consent form, please see Chapter 6, page 62.

Preparing this list of arrival tasks not only defines what needs to be done to get ready for the focus groups, but also defines who does what. For example, first June made a list of the arrival tasks. Then, she divided the tasks between Mary (the comoderator), Lisa (the note taker), and herself (the moderator). June's list of arrival tasks for her focus groups is presented in the box on page 83.

June's Tasks for Setting Up the Room

Mary
 Clear the bulletin board.
 Set up and test recording equipment.
 Make arrangements to turn off the PA system in the room.

June
 Set up food and drinks.
 Set up other materials (agenda, name tags, etc.).

What Should Be Said at the Beginning of the Focus Group?

Certainly, a mélange of several factors gives rise to a successful focus group. However, it is not an oversimplification to say that this success hinges on what a moderator conveys to the participants during the first 10 minutes of the focus group. For a focus group discussion to be productive, the moderator must set the tone for the entire focus group during the critical first 10 minutes. In a good, productive focus group discussion,

- The participants are at ease and contribute to the discussion without much prodding from the moderator.
- The participants listen to each other and respect the opinions of others.
- The participants talk to each other rather than only to the moderator.

Cross-Reference Tip
To learn more about what a moderator can say and do to control participant dynamics during the focus group, please see Chapter 9, page 101.

For such dynamics to take place, what is said to the participants at the beginning of the focus group is of great importance. Therefore we suggest that an outline for beginning the focus group be developed so the correct terms and phrases are used while talking to the participants. Although it is important to be consistent across focus groups in what is said, note that the moderator should not sound as if he is reading from a script. Instead, the moderator should know the outline well enough to say what needs to be said in a conversational tone. The outline should include the following eight elements:

June's List of Arrival Tasks for Parent Focus Groups

Lisa

   Greet participants at the door (main entrance).
   Thank them for coming.
   Direct them to the room.

Mary

   Greet participants.
   Direct them to the name tags and pen. Tell them to put on a name
      tag (first names only).
   Direct them to the table.

June

   Greet participants.
   Have them complete the participant consent form.

1. Introduce and explain the roles of the moderator and comoderator.
Here, the moderator and the comoderator introduce themselves and explain their roles. This is necessary so the participants are not distracted or
offended by what the moderator or the comoderator is doing. For example,
a participant might wonder about a comoderator who is taking notes, "Oh!
I wonder what she is doing? Is she writing something about me?" or about
the moderator who is looking at his watch, "Great! He is looking at his
watch. He must be bored by what I am saying. I better shut up."

2. Thank the participants for coming. The goal here is to communicate
to the participants the importance of their contributions. It is essential to
convey to them that the moderator and the comoderator are there to learn
from them.

3. Clarify the purpose of the focus group. It is easy for the participants
to contribute and stay on the topic if they clearly understand the purpose of
the focus group. All technical terms must be clarified and the limitations of
the discussion must be explained.

4. Clarify how the time will be spent. The purpose of this feature is to
inform the participants of the duration of the focus group and if and when a
break will be taken. Participants can be encouraged to stay focused by being reminded of the time limits and of the task at hand.

5. Provide a description of the participants. The task here is to convey to the participants who they are and why they have been selected. Participants may feel more comfortable when they know that they have all been selected for the same reason. This sense of commonality may help them in sharing their ideas.

6. Explain protocol for addressing each other. The norm is to use first names only for all those present (i.e., moderator, comoderator, and participants). This makes the session more informal.

7. Have the participants introduce themselves and conduct an ice-breaker activity. An ice-breaker is an activity or a question designed to build rapport and to "warm up" or "loosen up" the participants.

8. Explain ground rules for participating in the discussion. The purpose of this feature is to set the tone for participant discussion, as noted in the previous paragraph. Participants are made aware not only of the behaviors that are acceptable and desired but also of the behaviors that are unacceptable.

June incorporated all of the above elements as she worked on how to begin the focus groups. June's plan is presented in the box on page 86.

What Are the Main Questions?

The main questions of a focus group arise out of the purpose of the project and are designed to elicit information from the participants to meet the objectives of the project. Main questions are broad, open-ended questions designed to open up the discussion. It takes roughly 15 to 20 minutes to address each of these questions sufficiently. On an average, there are around two to four questions per focus group; however, some focus groups may have only one question, whereas some may have as many as six.

The task here is to develop the main questions to guide the focus group discussion. This task requires you to make decisions on the following issues:

- How many questions should I use?
- How should I word these questions?
- How should I sequence these questions?

As you proceed with the task, remember to take into account the purpose statement and the objectives of the project as well as the estimated length of the focus group. Also, keep in mind the time needed for each question (15-20 minutes) when deciding how many questions to include. As for the sequence of the questions, this determination is essential for two rea-

Examples of Ice-Breakers

- Please tell us what grade level your child is in. Also, please tell us one thing about yourself or your child.
- Please tell us why you agreed to participate in the focus group.
- Please tell us—in one sentence—your most memorable experience when you were an elementary, middle, or high school student.
- Please tell us the one thing you remember about your favorite teacher.
- If you were to repeat one grade, which grade would it be and why?
- If you could trade places with a nationally known person for one day, who would it be and why?
- Compared to your school days, what is the one thing that is the most different about your life today?

sons. One, it helps the moderator control the discussion and stay focused on the topic. Two, it helps in analyzing the findings because information on a topic is not scattered throughout the focus group discussion.

The task of developing focus group questions takes time to accomplish. Usually, more than one draft is necessary to make the questions simple, clear, and concise. You can be more productive at this task by working with another individual or individuals. Keep in mind the following guidelines as you prepare the questions:

- Questions should be one-dimensional. For example, consider the following question: "What are your problems and concerns?" Problems and concerns may be interpreted as two separate issues. So, the question should use only problems or only concerns.
- Questions should be open-ended (for example, "What do you think about the school policy on homework?") instead of closed-ended (for example, "Do you think the school policy on homework is good or bad?"). Open-ended questions help open up the discussion. Please note though, that some seemingly open-ended questions are not truly open-ended; such questions have qualifiers attached that require participants to answer within a range. For example, asking participants, "How concerned are you about the school's homework policy?" would be less likely to open up the discussion than asking a truly open-ended question such as "What concerns do you have about the school's homework policy?"
- Avoid "piggybacking" the questions: That is, do not attach one question to another. A string of questions is usually confusing to the participants. For example, don't ask, "What are your expectations of the school? What kind of policy would you like to see?" Instead, pose just one of these questions at a time.

June's Plan for Beginning a Parent Focus Group

Outline	Example wording
(June starts here) Introduce: Self Mary Lisa	Hello, I'm June. I'll be moderating the discussion tonight. This is Mary, who will be helping me with the discussion, especially by helping me stay on track! You may see Mary and me write down some notes as we go along, but mainly we'll rely on the next person I'd like to introduce, Lisa, to take notes.
Thank you: How chosen:	Thank you for taking the time to come. All of you here are parents of Snyder Elementary students and were randomly selected from the school directory. We are here to learn from you because you are the people who can tell us how things look from a parent's viewpoint.
Tonight's purpose:	You all received an agenda in the mail. We have a great school here, but there is always room for improvement. We would like to make this school an even better place. So, our goal tonight is to identify areas for further improvement and growth.
(Mary takes over) Ice-breaker:	We'll be using just first names when speaking with one another tonight. Please introduce yourselves and tell us one special thing about one of your children. Would anyone like to start? Thanks [person's name], after you've introduced yourself, we can go around the table.
Time limit, restate agenda/purpose:	We will have about an hour and a half for our discussion tonight; we'll be taking a brief break about halfway through. Given our time constraints, I'll ask everyone to stay on the topic so we can address the task at hand: to identify areas for further improvement and growth of Snyder Elementary.
(June takes over) Requests to help us (ground rules):	Besides staying on the topic, there are some other ways you can help. First, we want to hear from all of you—no matter how trivial your comment may be to you, it may be important information for us. Also, please take turns while talking. If two of you talk at once, the rest of us may not be able to hear everything that is said. One of the most important things to remember is to speak your mind—we want to know what your actual opinions are on the topic. The more ideas we hear tonight, the better. We're not here to evaluate any ideas or to come to a consensus; besides, there are no right or wrong ideas anyway.
About looking at watch:	Finally, a couple of other things: Feel free to ask questions of each other—I don't need to be the only one who asks questions! Also, if you see me look at my watch, please don't think I'm impolite—I'll just be trying to keep us on schedule.

- Main questions need not always be formatted in question form. For example, instead of "What are the characteristics of an ideal school?" you could format the same query as a command statement or as an incomplete sentence. You would then say, "Please tell us your idea of an ideal school" or "My idea of an ideal school is ____."

A School District's Focus Group Questions

A school district—wanting to provide a 21st-century education for its students—asked its staff, faculty, business community, higher education officials, parents, and students about new and improved programming at its three high schools and the planned fourth one.

1. What challenges/changes do you see facing students graduating from high school in the 21st century?
2. As you look to the future, what would you like to see implemented to improve our high school programs? This is your wish list.
3. What innovative area(s) of study would expand opportunities for students?
4. If you could implement one new academic or program idea in our high schools, what would it be?
5. If any of these ideas shared in our session today were implemented, what do you think would be the specific benefits for our students (such as time, earning, student learning, future employment, productivity, workforce needs, etc.)?
6. Is there one comment, about enhancing student education for the future, you would like to make that was not covered by this discussion?

SOURCE (for list only): Olathe District 21st-Century High School Steering Team, 2001. Reprinted with permission.

- The main questions need not be completely mutually exclusive of each other. Often, the questions overlap with each other to some degree, but this is not a problem as long as the overlapping question results in additional information from participants. To illustrate this point, in the box above, we have included the questions used by a school district in their focus group project. You will note that question numbers two, three, and six overlap.

June took all these guidelines into account while developing her questions. Her questions are presented in the box on page 88.

What Are the Areas for Probing?

After developing the questions, the next task is to identify the areas that would have to be probed further during the focus group discussion. By identifying the areas of importance ahead of time, it is possible to keep the

June's Main Questions

1. What are some of the areas that are in need of improvement at the school?
2. What suggestions do you have to address these needs?

discussion focused. Another advantage of giving the focus group discussion some forethought is that it is possible to identify alternate ways of saying the same thing to get at the same information. Here, you might identify some key words and phrases that could trigger additional comments from the participants. The areas June identified for probing during the discussion are described in the box on page 89.

How Can a Focus Group Discussion Be Monitored?

It is essential to monitor the focus groups while conducting them, to make sure everything that needs to be done has been done. Another advantage of monitoring focus groups is that it helps to ensure that the same message is being conveyed, the same questions are being asked, and the same tasks are being performed and completed in the proper sequence, across all focus groups. Maintaining such consistency makes the findings more believable and trustworthy. It is especially crucial to have such confidence in the findings when high-stakes decisions are being considered. High-stakes decisions essentially involve major changes that affect many people and require enormous amounts of time, effort, and resources.

One way of monitoring focus groups is to develop a checklist of all the critical tasks that need to be done before, during, or after the discussion. Because the moderator will have his or her hands full with the task of conducting the focus group, it is ordinarily the responsibility of the comoderator to keep track of the focus group events by using the checklist. However, in some projects, moderators may be conducting focus groups by themselves, without the help of comoderators. In these circumstances, the responsibility of filling out the checklist falls on the moderators. They will be otherwise occupied during the focus group but can complete the checklist during the break and after the focus group is over.

Because June was able to secure the assistance of a comoderator, she planned to keep track of the focus group by the completion of a checklist. She developed the checklist shown in Form 8.1 and assigned the responsibility for completing it to Mary, the comoderator. Note that in the last column, "During Focus Group," June identified a number of tasks that are

June's Areas for Probing

- What are some of the areas that need improvement at the school?
  Ask about dissatisfaction with something from the present.
  Ask about dissatisfaction with something from the past.
  Try alternate words: *concerns, expectations, likes, dislikes.*
  Ask specifically about environmental concerns.
  Ask specifically about commercialization of schools.

- What suggestions do you have to address these needs?
  Be sure to address the issues raised by the participants in response
    to the first main question.
  Ask for suggestions to address the two specific issues (environmen-
    tal concerns and commercialization).
  Try alternate words or phrases: *solutions, recommendation for
    improving.*

essential to effectively moderating the focus group. These tasks relating to effective moderation are covered in depth in Chapter 9.

How Are Focus Group Guides Tested?

The focus group guide should be tested so that you can get feedback on the clarity, comprehensiveness, and appropriateness of the guide. Suggestions for testing the focus group guide, in terms of who can give feedback and how it can be done, are provided in Table 8.1.

June tested the focus group guide in two ways. First, she gave it to two colleagues, Mary and Lisa. June asked for their opinions about the clarity of the wording, the suitability of the language with respect to the participants, and the depth and breadth of the guide. Then, she asked two other parents to stay a few minutes after a PTA meeting one evening. She read the outline for beginning the focus group and asked them what they thought of it. Then, she asked them to respond to the focus group questions. On the basis of their answers, she was able to determine whether each question could be easily understood. After considering the feedback she got from the parents, she used their suggestions to make some changes in the guide.

In summary, we would like to emphasize one point in particular: Conducting focus groups requires forethought and preparation. Even if you have experience in conducting focus groups, you will still need to think through and prepare for each focus group project. If you are a novice, this planning and getting ready ahead of time will enable you to moderate the focus group well despite your lack of experience.

Form 8.1. June's Checklist for Monitoring Focus Groups

Date _____   Participants _____   Topic _____

Time begin _____   Time end _____

Moderator: June   Comoderator: Mary   Note taker: Lisa

Directions: Check all areas as they are completed.

Before Focus Group	**Start Focus Group**	**During Focus Group**
Mary ❏ Cleared bulletin board ❏ Set up and tested recording equipment ❏ Turned off PA system **June** ❏ Set up food and drinks ❏ Set up other materials (agenda, name tags, etc.) **Arrival tasks—Lisa and Mary** ❏ Directed participants to room ❏ Confirmed attendance list ❏ Handed out agendas ❏ Handed out name tags **June** ❏ Greeted participants individually ❏ Explained use of tape recorder **Mary** ❏ Turned on recorder at _____ o'clock	**June** ❏ Introduced self, Mary, and Lisa ❏ Thanked participants for coming ❏ Described how participants were chosen ❏ Explained purpose of focus group **Mary** ❏ Conducted ice-breaker activity ❏ Reemphasized time limits and agenda for session **June** ❏ Explained ground rules for discussion ❏ Explained looking-at-watch behavior	**June** ❏ Asked the question as planned ❏ Reminded participants when 2 minutes remained **Lisa** ❏ Took notes **June and Mary** ❏ Paraphrased/summarized responses ❏ Asked participants to clarify/correct summary ❏ Maintained verbal and nonverbal neutrality ❏ Gave everyone a chance to speak ❏ Did not ask leading probes ❏ Stated probes mostly as commands rather than questions ❏ Stated probes mostly in open-ended form **Mary** ❏ Turned off tape recorder at _____ o'clock

Table 8.1   Testing a Focus Group Guide

Feedback Source	What Should They Do?	What Should You Look For?
Individuals from the participant group (for example, if some parent focus groups are to be conducted, ask some parents who will not be taking part in the focus groups to give some feedback)	• Ask the individuals to look over the outline and check for clarity and appropriateness of the words and of the message being conveyed in the outline.	• Did they have trouble understanding any phrases or words? • Are they offended by anything?
	• Ask the individuals to look over the questions and check for clarity and appropriateness of the words in the questions.	• Did they understand the questions?
	• Ask the individuals to respond to the main questions. (This can be done on a one-on-one basis or in a group.)	• Do their answers contain the type of information you are seeking? • Are their answers off topic? • Do the answers reflect misunderstanding of certain phrases or words?
Colleagues	• Ask them to look over the entire guide.	• Did they identify anything I have forgotten and need to add?

At a Glance: Developing a Focus Group Guide

❏ Have I developed a list of items I need for the focus group?
❏ Have I collected and/or purchased those items?
❏ Have I identified the tasks that need to be done to set up the room?
❏ Have I delineated and communicated responsibility for those tasks?
❏ Have I identified what needs to be done as the participants arrive?
❏ Have I delineated and communicated responsibility for those tasks?
❏ Have I developed the outline for the beginning of the focus group?
❏ Have I communicated that outline to the comoderator?
❏ Have I developed the main questions?
❏ Have I identified areas for probing?
❏ Have I developed a checklist for monitoring focus groups?
❏ Have I tested the focus group guide?
❏ Have I made any necessary changes?

9

Moderating a Focus Group

Chapter at a Glance

- What are the phases of a focus group?
- How should the focus group begin?
- How can participant responses for each question be initiated?
- How can participants be probed?
- How can closure be obtained for each question?
- How can problem participants be managed?
- How should the focus group end?
- Why must everyone conducting a focus group meet immediately afterward?
- What is the most challenging part of the task of moderating a focus group?
- What are some do's and don'ts of moderating?
- Why is it essential to conduct a "test" focus group?
- What training do moderators need?

Moderating a focus group is a not a difficult task to learn, but it is certainly a challenging task to perform. Although the responsibilities of moderating a focus group can leave any moderator mentally exhausted, it may be more pronounced for novice moderators due to their lack of experience. Moderating skills improve with the amount of practice or experience a moderator has had, and a novice can strive for successful experiences by meticulously planning and preparing for the focus groups.

The purpose of this chapter is to suggest some techniques for moderating focus groups. The moderating style suggested here is a directive and structured way of conducting focus groups. A structured style of moderating focus groups helps in maintaining procedural consistency across focus groups and moderators. Remember, by procedural consistency, we mean making sure that the same message is being conveyed, the same questions are being asked, and the same tasks are being performed in the same sequence across all focus groups in a given project.

Here is one final note on the structured style of moderating focus groups. We believe that the structured style of moderating focus groups is more suited for use in schools for two reasons: School projects are more likely to use novice moderators and are also more likely to involve more than one moderator. The cost constraints in schools necessitate that most focus group projects be handled by inexperienced in-house moderators rather than by a highly experienced, but costly, external moderator. Furthermore, given the workload demands on the individuals working at schools, focus group projects may in reality be handled by more than one in-house person. Thus the structured style of conducting focus groups will enable a group of novice moderators to conduct focus groups in a consistent manner and thus lend credibility to the information they gather. As a final note, it is essential to remember that style and technique alone will not result in successful experiences. The moderator's infectious enthusiasm and desire to learn are also important factors and make it more likely that participants will be eager and helpful.

What Are the Phases of a Focus Group?

A focus group has three distinct phases: the beginning, the discussion, and the ending. During the beginning phase, the moderators and participants introduce themselves and the moderator explains how the discussion itself will be conducted. During the discussion phase, each of the main questions is discussed in the predetermined order and the moderator probes as needed. During the ending phase, the moderator gives participants an opportunity for final questions and comments and then concludes the session. In the sections following, we describe how to go about conducting each of these phases effectively.

How Should the Focus Group Begin?

Once the participants and the moderator are seated around the table, the focus group can begin. This phase of the focus group is usually 10 minutes in duration. The moderator begins the focus group by following the outline that was developed as a part of the focus group guide. Here, the moderator and comoderator introduce themselves and explain their roles during the focus group. The moderator also explains who all the participants are and why they have been selected. Thereafter, the moderator (a) clarifies the purpose of the focus group, how time will be spent, and the protocol for using first names when addressing each other; (b) asks the participants to introduce themselves; and (c) conducts an ice-breaker activity to get everyone "warmed up" or "loosened up." After the ice-breaker, the moderator explains the ground rules for participating in the discussion, asks the participants whether they have any questions or concerns, and addresses those areas before moving on to the discussion phase.

> **Cross-Reference Tip**
> To learn more about the outline for beginning the focus group, please see Chapter 8, page 81.

How Can Participant Responses for Each Question Be Initiated?

The moderator begins the discussion phase by asking the first main question. Remember, the order, the wording of the questions, and the time available for each main question has already been determined in the focus group guide. For each question, the moderator initially elicits responses from every participant in the group by going around the table. This procedure is also referred to as calling on the participants, polling, or going around in a round-robin format. Going around the table and asking each participant to respond to a question serves two important functions. It reinforces what was said to the participants at the beginning of the group—that everyone's contribution is needed and important. It also ensures that everyone is heard from in the limited time frame and encourages the reticent ones to participate. Here are some tips to make this a successful activity.

> **Cross-Reference Tip**
> To learn more about the main questions, please see Chapter 8, page 84.

- Remember to give the participants a minute or two to collect their thoughts if an advance organizer was not provided.
- Ask for someone to volunteer initially; then, go around the table eliciting answers from the remaining volunteers. It is better to have a confident participant volunteer than to call on a shy one.
- Accept all participants' comments without displaying any judgment regarding quality.
- Listen to all participants' comments before calling on individuals to clarify or elaborate. This will give you a range of opinions, and you will know what to expect from each participant and how much to probe each participant.
- Finally, don't let the same individual answer all the questions first. Have a different person start each time. This will prevent the other participants from being influenced and guided by one person's agenda.

How Can Participants Be Probed?

Cross-Reference Tip
To learn more about the areas for probing, please see Chapter 8, page 87.

After the initial structure described above, the moderator opens up the discussion so it is less rigid and more spontaneous. The goal here is to get the participants to engage in a discussion by addressing one another–rather than only the moderator–with their comments and questions. During this open discussion, the moderator ensures that there is parity in participant contributions, steers and guides the discussion toward relevant and sought-after areas, and probes the participants. Remember, these relevant and sought-after areas have already been determined in the focus group guide.

Probing is an integral part of the task of moderating a focus group. Probing means asking questions or making comments to stimulate or extract information from the participants or to clarify, elaborate, or fine-tune what was previously said by the participants. (Remember not to confuse probing questions with the main focus group questions discussed in the previous section and in Chapter 8.) More specifically, probing helps do the following:

- Stimulate a waning discussion by generating new topics for discussion
- Extract information from reticent or reserved participants
- Clarify participants' comments to prevent misunderstanding or misinterpretation
- Elaborate participants' comments by adding breadth and depth
- Fine-tune the discussion by eliminating certain unwanted topics and focusing attention on the topics of interest

See Table 9.1 for some suggestions on how probes can be used during the discussion.

Another way that moderators sometimes probe participants is to initially ask questions such as "How many of you feel the same way?" or "How many of you have experienced this?" and then ask for a show of hands to get an idea of where the group stands. Although this can be an acceptable practice for stimulating discussion, you will need to keep in mind that numerical information such as hand counts should not later be used to "sum up" the discussion. For example, even if half of the parents in a focus group want the new math program, you will have absolutely no idea what proportion of all the parents in the school want it.

Also note that when participants are selected and screened judiciously, you will usually get participants who have some things to discuss. This makes the task of probing much easier; stimulating and extracting information from the participants should not be like pulling teeth. But sometimes, even with the best of your moderating skills, some focus groups will just not go the way you want them to. The group dynamics may be very sluggish, and the participants may take time to warm up or may not be very talkative. In such cases, the importance of effective probing is magnified.

Table 9.1   Examples of Probing Technique

Purpose	Suggestions
Stimulate	Use nonintrusive ways to encourage participation: • Use silence to your advantage: The best probe is sometimes no probe at all. Simply waiting for an answer helps those who are slower or uncertain to formulate their answers. Silence is also uncomfortable, and this may influence someone to talk. • Use encouraging cues, such as nods of the head, "Um-hums," and eye contact. When the topic is uncomfortable or personal, discuss the issue in terms of an experience of another person: • How do you think another person (e.g., parent, teacher) would feel in this situation? Encourage a sluggish, waning discussion in creative ways: • Tell participants to write on index cards a single idea or ideas that come to their minds regarding the issue being discussed (no names on card). Collect the cards. Read each item aloud and discuss. • Call on each participant to obtain his or her response. • Take a break, confer with your comoderator, and restrategize. Call it quits if new efforts fail. When the participants begin to repeat each other, make it socially acceptable to differ: • Does anyone feel differently? • That's one point of view; how about another? Encourage participants' contributions with probes such as the following: • Is there anything else you want to say about _____? • If you could change only one thing, what would it be? • What is the one thing that bothers you the most? Avoid asking leading probes that limit and influence participants' responses: • Instead of saying, "This plan for the open house looks good, doesn't it?" say, "What do you think of this plan for the open house?"
Extract	It is better to initially use less intrusive probing techniques. State that you want to hear from those who haven't yet contributed. Give the reticent or reserved ones a chance to volunteer before calling on them: • We have heard from many of you. Thanks. Now we would like to hear from those who haven't had a chance yet to voice their feelings. Darcy, Tim, Mike, which one of you would like to go first? Call on the reticent or reserved participants when they fail to volunteer: • John, we haven't heard from you yet on this issue. Where do you stand? • Mike, I am interested in your thoughts on that. What is your experience like? • José, we would like to hear from you, too. Don't let the participants get away with short uninformative responses such as, "I agree" or "I have nothing new to add" or "It was just like the way Mike described." Expect the participants to say why they feel as they do or share their experiences: • Laurie, I'm interested in your reasons for agreeing. Could you share some experiences that will help us understand why you feel the way you do? • Joe, it looks as if you agree with Mike's point of view. Can you share some of your reasons with us, please?
Clarify	Obtain clarifications by reiterating, summarizing, and/or asking for experiences and examples: • Darcy, please help me here. I don't know whether I understood what you meant. • Paraphrase a participant's comment and say, "Have I got that right?" or "Have I summarized it correctly?" • Joe, can you please clarify that for me by sharing an experience? • Tim, you said that more phones would alleviate the situation. Could you give me an example of how phones could help? Avoid asking "Why?" questions because it may make the participants defensive: • Instead of saying, "John, you said that you did not like the open house very much. Why?" say, "John, what is it about the open house that you did not like?" or say, "How did you come to that decision?"

(continued)

Table 9.1   Continued

Purpose	Suggestions
Elaborate	Ask participants to elaborate on their comments by asking for more information or asking them to share an experience or an example: • That's an interesting observation, Joe. Can you elaborate a bit? • Sue, I would like to hear more about it. • Mary, please tell us what happened to make you believe as you do. • Emma, please tell us how that came to be. • Andrea, could you give me some more details? Remember to word your probe carefully if you want the participants to elaborate only on specific issues: • Judy, tell us more about your experience. I want to specifically hear about the ways they communicated with you. • Elaine, you said that you were dissatisfied with the magnet program because it had created two parallel schools under one roof. How did that happen? • Sue, you said that the school is not a safe place. Tell us what you saw or heard that makes you think that the school is unsafe. • Darcy, you said that you were disappointed with the way the front office staff dealt with you. Please tell us what happened when you spoke to them.
Fine-tune	Use probes to steer, guide, and narrow the focus of discussion: • Excuse me folks, I need to stop things because we are straying from our topic. We are here to discuss how you feel about school uniforms and not about in-school suspensions. Joe, you said a few minutes ago that the way kids dress doesn't have anything to do with how they act. Let's take off from there. Any other ideas about that? • The discussion has veered toward making recommendations for increasing racial tolerance. We are here to discuss the problems only at this time. Some of the problems we have identified are students sitting only with others of the same cultural group in the lunchroom, and harassing of interracial couples. Any others?

How Can Closure Be
Obtained for Each Question?

It is necessary to move on to the next question when the participants start to echo the responses of each other or when the allocated time for each question is about to run out. At this point, the moderator informs the participants of the remaining time (for example, 5 minutes) and gets closure for that question. The goals of the closure activity are to give the participants one final opportunity to contribute and to give the moderator one final chance to obtain clarifications. These dual goals can be met as the moderator summarizes what the group has said and asks one last time for clarifications and contributions. Then, the moderator moves on to the next question and the pattern we have described—initiating responses, probing during the ensuing discussion, obtaining closure for the question—is repeated until all the questions are addressed.

How Can Problem
Participants Be Managed?

When conducting a focus group, the role that is probably least desirable to you is that of disciplinarian. But sometimes, the presence of certain participants or the dynamics of a group may necessitate that you be firm. Although you won't actually tell an individual to "be quiet," you will need to learn how to essentially get that message across. For instance, you may encounter the following behavior:

- An overzealous, exuberant participant who wants to share at the expense of what other participants have to say
- An overbearing participant who keeps interrupting others
- A rude participant who is judgmental and insulting of other participants
- Two or more individuals having a conversation among themselves
- A group that is very talkative and keeps wandering off topic

When dealing with such problems, always proceed from least intrusive to most intrusive methods for managing them. Take care not to interrupt the flow of the conversation or disturb the amicable atmosphere in the room. You must draw a balance: Step in as needed for unruly participants without making everyone else feel uncomfortable. You will not get a productive discussion if participants are ill at ease.

How Should the Focus Group End?

Moderators must take care not to prolong focus groups beyond their allotted time. They should therefore begin concluding sessions before the allotted time is about to run out. The moderator can start by informing the participants of the remaining time (5-10 minutes) and letting them know that it is time to conclude the focus group session. It is just about inevitable that some issues raised by participants during a focus group will not be adequately discussed. This may happen due to time constraints or because some issues mentioned by participants may not be relevant to the purpose of the focus group session. If this is the case, it is best for the moderator to acknowledge the situation. After that, the moderator asks whether the participants have any questions or concerns and addresses them. One question frequently raised by the participants is about the findings of the focus group or the focus group project on the whole. The participants may want to know whether these findings will be made available to them. You will

Suggestions for Managing Participants

Remind participants about the ground rules:
- "We want to hear from everyone. Joe, Tim, and Mike have shared some interesting information. Who would like to go next?"
- "Please refrain from making judgments. It is not our task tonight to determine the quality of these ideas."
- "We really need your help here. It is hard for us to understand and take notes when all of you talk at the same time. So, please one at a time."
- When people engage in side conversations, address a reminder to the whole group about everyone needing to hear every contribution.

Remind participants of the amount of time left and the questions that still need to be covered. Redirect participants as often as needed:
- "Folks, we keep digressing to the issue of ____. We are here only to discuss ____."

Try subtle ways:
- Avoid eye contact.
- Turn away from the person.
- Establish eye contact and simultaneously use your hands in the "Stop" pose.
- Change your seat. Sit next to the person instead of opposite.

Use humor to cut in and redirect the participants:
- Wave hands and say, "Ladies and gentlemen, remember me?"
- Tap on the table and say, "Whoaa! I wish I had my gavel with me now."

Address the individual or individuals directly:
- "Will you hold that thought for a minute, Darcy? I want to hear the rest of what Susan is saying."
- "Emma, you have been very forthcoming with your experiences. I would like to hear more from you. But we are on a tight schedule here. So, I would like to listen to someone else now."
- "Here, here. Let's listen to Jane now."
- "Sue, Robin, would you like to add anything?"

Use drastic measures:
- Change seats. Instead of sitting opposite, sit next to the difficult participant and avoid eye contact.
- Take a break. Thank the participant for contributing. Give the remuneration. Let the individual go.
- Reseat participants at break time to stop them from carrying on a conversation.

need to make a decision ahead of time on this issue and be prepared to follow through. Next, the moderator provides the participants with a contact number if they wish to speak to someone regarding the focus group. Finally, the moderator gives the participants the remunerations (when applicable) and thanks them for taking the time to participate in the focus group and for providing valuable assistance. The focus group then comes to an end.

Why Must Everyone Conducting a Focus Group Meet Immediately Afterward?

All focus group personnel (moderator, comoderator, and note taker) must meet immediately after conducting a focus group. The purpose of this post-focus-group meeting is threefold. One reason for conducting this meeting is to identify and summarize the salient points or features of the discussion as perceived by the moderator and the comoderator. Here, the moderator and the comoderator identify the issues they think were most important or poignant. The second reason for conducting a post-focus-group meeting is to evaluate the session to determine whether everything went according to plan and whether anything needs to be changed. This determination can best be made using the focus group monitoring checklist. The third reason for conducting the post-focus-group meeting is to identify information that needs to be shared with other moderators and comoderators. This is done to alert the others of possible problematic situations and to prevent them from committing the same mistakes.

It is essential to conduct the post-focus-group meeting immediately following the focus group when the information is still fresh. If the focus group session ends late in the evening and the moderator and the comoderator are tired, then it can wait until the following day but should be done first thing in the morning. Also, remember to tape-record the debriefing session so you don't have to take extensive notes.

What Is the Most Challenging Part of the Task of Moderating a Focus Group?

Perhaps the hardest part of the task of moderating a focus group is to simultaneously process the tasks of listening, watching, thinking, and monitoring. A moderator has to be not only completely immersed in the discussion but also on top of things all the time for a focus group to be productive. For instance, the moderator has to perform these tasks:

- Listen to the participants' comments
- Watch the body language of the participants
- Keep in mind which participants and which comments to come back to for probing
- Think of probes to use
- Monitor participants for parity in contributions
- Keep track of time to ensure that issues arising from the discussion and remaining questions can be addressed

Cross-Reference Tips

To learn more about scheduling focus groups, please see Chapter 5, page 53.

To learn more about the need for and the responsibilities of a comoderator, please see Chapter 6, page 55.

It is obvious that the moderator has to be mentally alert to engage in the above-mentioned activities concurrently. The demands of the task are magnified when a comoderator is not present. In those cases, the moderator will not have anyone to give a helping hand with the discussion. Furthermore, the moderator will have to shoulder some additional responsibilities, such as keeping an eye on the tape recorder and completing the checklist for monitoring the focus groups. For these reasons, we have suggested that no more than one focus group be conducted per day per moderator and that a comoderator be used whenever possible.

What Are Some Do's and Don'ts of Moderating?

Here are some additional tips and suggestions to make the task of moderating a successful experience:

- The moderator should operate the tape recorder during the session as well as after the session is over. Participants' "by the way" remarks may still provide valuable information.
- There should be no observers in a focus group because their presence may inhibit participation.
- The moderator can also encourage the quiet ones to participate more often by changing seats during the break. For example, instead of sitting next to the quiet ones, the moderator can sit opposite them to have better eye contact.
- A moderator conducting more than one focus group, often by the third group, begins to hear the same information. As a result, the moderator may start getting bored and inattentive and may miss relevant remarks. Therefore it is critical that moderators approach every focus group as if it were their first, with the same enthusiasm and desire for listening and learning from the participants.
- The moderator should appear to be one among the participants; he or she should not be perceived as an authority figure or expert. There are several ways to present this image of being a peer. The moderator's

Attending to Body Language

Participant's Behavior	*Moderator's Response*
Nodding head in agreement	John, I see you nodding. What is your experience?
Shaking head from side to side	Mary, what is your position on this?
Frowning	Steve, I see you frowning. Is there something you disagree with?
Opening mouth, but unable to cut in	Darcy, would you like to add something?

conduct is one way—for instance, sitting along the side of the table and not at the head of the table as an authority figure would. Certainly, the moderator should never be condescending or patronizing toward the participants. Manner of dress is another way to achieve the image of a being a peer. The moderator's clothing should not project an image of authority. The goal is to make the participants comfortable, so it is essential to keep things simple and wear casual clothing in most cases. Another rule of thumb is to consider how the participants are likely to dress and then choose your own clothing accordingly. For instance, if the participants will be administrators of a school, it would be fine to be more professionally dressed.

- The basic premise behind the focus group discussion is that participants will speak their mind within the comfort and security of a group. The moderator encourages this candor using strategies we have previously described. Despite these efforts, there may be some participants who may never feel comfortable in a group. Consequently, they may not be completely candid and may even withhold information that could be relevant to the project. One way of overcoming this limitation is to switch off the tape recorder toward the end of the discussion to see whether the participants contribute anything new. Another way of overcoming this limitation is to give the participants a writing task before ending the focus group. The task should take no more than a few minutes to complete. The participants should be told not to write their names on their response sheets. The stimulus for a writing task should be a question that relates to the main purpose of the focus group. Some examples of stimulus questions include the following:

> List five ways in which you would address this problem.
> What is the most important problem according to you?
> Tell us about something we have not discussed that you think is
>   important or relevant to the topic.

Why Is It Essential to
Conduct a "Test" Focus Group?

A "test" focus group is, in essence, the very first focus group that is conducted with the actual participants. It is essential to conduct a test focus group for two reasons. One reason is to determine whether any major changes have to be made to the manner in which the focus group will be conducted. You will need to pay special attention to the location and room arrangement, the arrival tasks, and the beginning of the focus group. You will also need to examine the moderator's probing techniques as well as the number, sequence, and wording of questions. If a significant number of changes have to be made, the information gathered from the focus group would have to be set aside and could not be included in the focus group findings. On the other hand, if everything went satisfactorily during the first focus group, the information gathered would be part of the focus group findings.

Another reason for conducting the test focus group is to determine whether the information gathered is satisfactory. The question to be asked here is, "Did we get what we set out to get?" If not, then the purpose of the focus group obviously needs to be revisited. This should not really happen if sufficient attention has been paid to the task of clarifying the purpose at the beginning of the focus group project. Yet there is no harm in double-checking and making sure that the information gathered is what you are looking for.

What Training Do Moderators Need?

What makes a novice moderator a skilled one? The answer is practice and experience. By first practicing and then actually going through the experience of moderating a focus group, you will gain valuable insights into the task. Knowing what to do does not always tell you what not to do. Therefore we recommend that you prepare, practice, err, and learn before you conduct a focus group that actually counts. Here are some suggestions for gaining that experience:

- Pair with another individual who is interested in conducting the focus groups. Critique each other's moderating skills.
- Practice mock focus groups. This can be done by gathering a group of people and conducting one or more focus groups. Participants for these mock focus groups could be anyone, including potential participants who did not meet all the screening criteria or a group of parents or teachers who would be willing to role-play.

Form 9.1. Moderator's Self-Check

Compared to an ideal moderator, did I . . .

❏ Guide the discussion toward the purpose and objectives of the focus group project and demonstrate thorough knowledge of the topic?
❏ Put the participants at ease and encourage them to candidly share their ideas?
❏ Use good questioning and probing skills?
❏ Express my thoughts, ideas, and questions clearly?
❏ Maintain a neutral stance?
❏ Listen patiently?
❏ Attend to subtle nonverbal language (body language, tone of voice, signs of tension)?
❏ Anticipate possible comments from participants and plan ahead of time for the appropriate probes?
❏ Know when it was necessary to probe participants' comments further?
❏ Know when to follow a matter of importance?

As a final note, we want to expand on a point we made at the beginning of this chapter: For any moderator—novice or experienced—skills improve according to practice and experience. But actually, practice and experience alone do not maximize the degree of improvement. Rather, experience must be coupled with informed reflection and a commitment to keep fine-tuning your moderating skills. To that end, we encourage you to evaluate your skills on a continuing basis. One way to accomplish this is to use a checklist, such as the one shown in Form 9.1, to evaluate yourself after moderating a focus group.

At a Glance: Moderating a Focus Group

❏ Have I trained all the moderators?
❏ Have I conducted a "test" focus group?
❏ Have I made any necessary changes?

For each focus group that has been conducted,
❏ Have I completed the checklist for monitoring focus groups?
❏ Have I conducted a post-focus-group meeting after each focus group?
❏ Have I labeled and organized audiotapes, notes, and all other necessary material?
❏ Have I completed the moderator's self-check?

10

Analyzing and Reporting Focus Group Findings

Chapter at a Glance

- What are the guiding principles for analyzing focus group discussions?
- What are the stages of the analysis process?
- What decisions have to be made prior to analyzing?
- What are the procedures for analyzing each focus group discussion?
- What are the procedures for analyzing and interpreting findings from all the focus groups?
- What should be included in a focus group report?
- When is a written analysis or report unnecessary?

After you have conducted the focus groups planned for your project, you now face the task of analyzing the focus group discussions. At first thought, it may seem that you have already learned what you needed from the focus group project: The information you heard during a focus group may seem so apparent and obvious that analyzing it seems unnecessary. However, only systematic analysis will uncover the important information from the discussions. For a focus group project to be truly worthwhile, you will need to extract *all* the important information from the discussions rather than only the information that is most obvious and memorable. In reality, much of the important information is imbedded within the partici pants' conversation. Therefore the goals of analyzing focus group discussions are to weed through all the information gathered, to pick out the information that is directly related to the purposes of your project, and finally, to summarize and interpret the information.

Focus group projects can result in a significant amount of information because a lot is said during each focus group discussion. The more focus groups conducted for a project, the more overwhelming, daunting, and unappealing the task of analysis may be. The task may be especially daunting for individuals working in schools, given their time constraints and other responsibilities. It is true that analyzing focus group discussions could turn out to be inordinately time-consuming. To make matters worse, the resulting analysis could turn out to be suspect if the analysis is completed in a haphazard and rushed manner. But before you get discouraged, be assured that there is an antidote to this dilemma, which is discussed in this chapter.

We believe that analysis of focus group information can be efficient and practical as well as accurate and trustworthy; we do *not* believe that you must sacrifice one goal for the other. Therefore the purpose of this final chapter is to provide some guidelines that will address both goals: to make the task of analyzing focus groups more practical and realistic and also to ensure the trustworthiness of the findings. Another objective of this chapter is to provide some guidelines on the final activity of the focus group project—writing a report—and to discuss instances when detailed analysis or reports are unnecessary.

What Are the Guiding Principles for Analyzing Focus Group Discussions?

As mentioned earlier, when analyzing focus groups in schools, two issues are of utmost concern: the practicality of the procedures employed for analysis and the trustworthiness of the findings derived from the analysis. The need for practicality is obvious given the demands placed on school personnel. Procedures for analyzing focus groups therefore need to be uncomplicated, easy to apply, and as efficient as possible. With respect to trustworthiness, we have emphasized this as an important issue throughout the book. We believe that focus groups can be important and useful sources of information for school decisions. But this is true only when you and others have reason to be confident that the findings are accurate. Confidence in focus group findings is only possible when procedures for analysis are thoughtfully chosen and religiously followed.

To address these important issues, we have identified six guiding principles as being fundamental to the process of analyzing focus groups. Following these principles will ensure that the analysis of information from your focus group project will achieve the goals of practicality as well as trustworthiness. These are the six guiding principles:

- **Use the same people who have been involved all along:** The people who will be involved in analyzing the focus group information should be the same people who have been involved throughout, especially those who have conducted the focus groups.

- **Maintain an open mind:** Every attempt must be made by those involved in the analysis to set aside their own views to avoid bias and produce an impartial analysis.

- **Determine systematic procedures:** Focus groups should be analyzed using prearranged, systematic, and structured procedures.

- **Follow procedures consistently:** The procedures should be followed with absolute consistency within a project; every individual must use the same procedures in the same way every time a focus group discussion is analyzed.

- **Apply procedures diligently:** Focus group information must be analyzed carefully and conscientiously. Therefore all individuals involved must be committed to giving the task sufficient time and attention.

- **Keep procedures as simple as is appropriate:** Procedures for analyzing focus groups need to be simple, easy to follow, and no more complicated than necessary.

What Are the Stages of the Analysis Process?

Analyzing the information gathered from a focus group project is a process that consists of several stages. The first stage is a decision-making stage: You decide *who* will do the analysis and *how* it will be done. The subsequent stages—procedures for the analysis itself—consist of first analyzing each focus group discussion separately and then combining the analyses of the various focus group discussions conducted during your project. Finally, you will interpret the findings. More specifically, the process of analyzing information from focus groups is a 5-stage process, as summarized below:

Stage 1: Make decisions before beginning the analysis.
- Decide who will analyze the focus group information.
- Decide which method of identifying relevant information is to be used.

Stage 2: Analyze each focus group discussion separately.
- Identify information that is relevant for each main question; set aside information that is not relevant to any of the main questions.
- Paraphrase the identified information in condensed form.

Avoiding Bias While Analyzing Focus Group Findings

To avoid bias, you must do the following:

- Keep an open mind: Assume that all information gathered is important and avoid exclusion of some information because you disagree with the contents or because it does not fit your preconceived notions.

- Avoid selective attention: That is, avoid attending only to some information instead of all of it because of your frame of reference. Krueger (1994) aptly illustrated the implications of selective attention with the following anecdote:

  > Two scientists had not seen each other since they were undergraduates at the university—15 years earlier. They were good friends but their careers led them to different parts of the world. One had become a herpetologist and traveled around the world studying snakes. Her friend became an ornithologist, and she conducted most of her research studying birds in the Amazon rainforest. Eventually their paths would cross again. The snake expert had to travel to Amazon en route to her next assignment and took the opportunity to visit her old friend. While they were visiting, they decided to walk together through a portion of rainforest. When they finished, the bird expert was excited because in 1 hour she had seen 18 varieties of birds, but she apologized to her friend for the lack of snakes. "What do you mean?" said her friend. "While we were walking, I saw 12 varieties of snakes." (p. 130)

FYI: Using Computer Software for Analyzing Focus Group Information

Computer software programs make some of the mechanical aspects of selecting and organizing information from focus group discussions more efficient and precise. In addition, these programs can make a more sophisticated analysis possible. This level of analysis, however, is beyond the scope of this book: We believe that the level of analysis enabled by software programs is more appropriate for researchers than for school personnel. However, if you want to know more about this option, *Computer Programs for Qualitative Data Analysis*, by Weitzman and Miles (1995), is an excellent source for descriptions and comparisons of 24 software programs.

- Place the condensed information under the main question to which it applies.
- Recheck the compiled information under each main question.

Stage 3: Combine information *within* each participant group.
- Collate the information from all focus groups from the same participant group.
- Organize the information so that information from all those focus groups is placed together under each main question.
- As needed, group the information under each main question into categories and subcategories.

Stage 4: Compare and contrast information *across* participant groups.
- Review the combined information from each participant group.
- Note similarities and differences across participant groups for each category under each main question.

Stage 5: Interpret the information from the entire focus group project.
- Review the analysis in light of the purpose of the focus group project.
- Describe how the focus group findings could or should influence any pending decisions.

> **Cross-Reference Tip**
> A participant group (e.g., parents, teachers, or students) is a segment of the population whose input is needed for the focus group project. For more information, see Chapter 4, pages 31-33.

What Decisions Have to Be Made Prior to Analyzing?

As outlined in the previous section, the first stage of the analysis process is a decision-making stage. Before actually analyzing the focus group information, you will make two decisions. You will first determine who will analyze the information. Second, you will select a method for identifying relevant information from the discussions. We explain these two decisions in the following paragraphs.

Decide Who Will Analyze the Focus Group Information. The task here is simply to determine who will analyze the focus group information. The first and best answer to that question is clear: the same individuals who conducted the focus group discussions. That is, the people most likely to be able to complete an accurate and useful analysis include the moderator, the comoderator, and the note taker. Furthermore, we recommend that the moderator take a lead role in analyzing the focus group information. The moderator has been involved throughout the project and is the person who can best provide consistency and a "deeper understanding" of the project.

Therefore the insight the moderator brings to the process of analysis will be invaluable.

Despite the advantages of moderators analyzing the focus group information, this arrangement may not always be feasible in the case of external moderators. If you have hired someone to conduct your focus groups, you may not have the resources to fund their leadership role in the analysis process. In such cases, there is another choice: the in-house person you assigned to oversee the project. Remember that in Chapter 2 we discussed the importance of an in-house designate who works alongside an external moderator as the focus groups are planned and conducted. This in-house designate is the next-best person to take the lead role in analyzing the focus group information if you cannot afford to keep the external moderator on board.

We have discussed who can best take a leadership role during the analysis process. For smaller focus group projects, that person might actually complete all the analysis single-handedly. Typically, though, practical and logistical issues will necessitate the task being shared among two or more individuals; those individuals would include the comoderator and the note taker in addition to the moderator. Note that in the case of a large focus group project with more than one moderator, the task would most likely be shared among the moderators. But regardless of who the individuals are, extra care needs to be taken whenever more than one person analyzes information from a focus group project. Those individuals must keep in mind the guiding principles discussed earlier in this chapter. In particular, they will need to pay close attention to the principles of maintaining consistency, working diligently, and keeping an open mind. Compromising any of these principles would surely affect the trustworthiness of the findings.

Decide on a Method for Identifying Relevant Information. Once you have decided who will analyze the focus group information, the next decision is to determine which method will be used for identifying relevant information from the focus group discussion. This relevant information can be gathered from written and/or audiotaped records of that discussion. More specifically, there are four ways in which relevant information can be gathered from written or audiotaped records of discussions:

Transcript, Transcribing, Transcriber
When a word-for-word written record is made of the contents of an audiotape, the resulting product is referred to as a transcript. The process of making the record is referred to as transcribing, and the person who makes it is referred to as a transcriber.

- Typed transcripts
- Audiotapes
- Notes plus audiotapes
- Notes only

These methods are compared and contrasted in Table 10.1. Clearly, there is no one best option; each method has certain advantages and disadvantages. Determining which method is most appropriate for a particular focus group project is a decision that can be made by considering the advantages and disadvantages of the methods in conjunction with certain other factors. Thus you can start the decision-making process by reflecting on the following questions:

Table 10.1 Stage 1: A Comparison of the Methods Used in Identifying Relevant Information

Method	Identifying Relevant Information			
	Typed Transcript	*Audiotapes*	*Notes Plus Audiotapes*	*Notes Only*
Is it time- and effort-intensive?	Most time and effort → This is a time- and effort-intensive procedure. It takes time to read the transcript, weed through participants' comments, and identify the relevant information (the average transcript length is 50 pages; the average time needed to analyze is 3 to 4 hours).	This method also takes time and effort because information has to be weeded through; but it is not as intensive as using a transcript (the average time needed to analyze is 2 to 3 hours).	Information is gathered mainly from the notes. Audiotapes are used only to gather quotations. Therefore it is not as time- and effort-intensive as the previous two methods.	← Least time and effort Turnaround time is the least.
Will the findings be detailed?	Most details The amount of detail that can be obtained cannot be duplicated by any other technique.	Less detailed than the transcript method but more than the other two methods.		Fewest details
Can quotations be gathered?	Yes	Yes	Yes	No
Will there be a delay in analyzing?	Yes It takes time to get the audiotapes transcribed. Therefore it is not possible to start analyzing the findings right after the focus group.	No	No	No
		No delay in analyzing the focus group findings.		
Will additional costs be incurred?	Yes Transcribing audiotapes can be expensive (a minimum of $20 per hour). An hour of audiotape takes 4 to 5 hours to transcribe.	No	No	No
		No transcribing costs associated with these methods.		
Is it possible to be aware of the emotions, mood, and innuendos of the participants during the analysis?	No A transcript is "cold." It is not possible to be completely aware of the depth of feeling present in participants' remarks. However, if a moderator is analyzing the manuscript, some of the emotional overtones could be recalled. Remember, this recall is subject to time.	Yes Audiotapes, regardless of when they are heard or who analyzes them, will always provide the emotional overtones.	Yes Because audiotapes will be heard to gather quotations, the emotional overtones will be heard.	No Notes are "cold," like a transcript; but, if a moderator is analyzing, his or her observations and impressions will be available. However, this recall is also subject to time.
Is a complete, easily accessible record of the focus group discussion available?	Yes Transcripts provide a permanent, easily accessible, complete record of the focus group discussion.	No The analyzer must go back to the audiotapes every time something needs to be checked.	No Notes do not provide a complete picture; the analyzer must go back to the audiotapes if the accuracy of a quotation needs to be checked.	No Notes do not provide a complete picture.

What are high-stakes decisions?
High-stakes decisions are those that affect many people or lead to changes requiring enormous amounts of time, effort, and resources.

- What do you intend to do with the findings?
- How much weight are you attaching to the findings?
- When making a decision, will the focus group findings be used alone or in conjunction with other information?
- Will focus group findings be used in making high-stakes decisions?
- How important is it to be certain that the findings are complete and detailed?
- How much manpower and money is available for the analysis?
- How much time do you have for analysis and report writing?

In some instances, the task of determining the method for identifying relevant information is simple and linear. But in other instances, the decision is made by taking a multitude of factors into account. Suppose you are planning to make a high-stakes decision (for example, selecting new curricula) and will use the focus group findings as the main source of information. Because you are going to attach a lot of weight to those findings, they should be complete and detailed. Clearly, identifying relevant information from notes or notes plus audiotapes would not be good options because these methods do not produce a complete and detailed picture. Because transcripts do allow for more detailed analysis, this method would be your obvious choice if you have sufficient resources. However, if you are short on money and manpower, the audiotape method might be the next-best choice. While your analysis would then be less detailed, you would still have a much more complete and detailed outcome than if you had used either the notes-only or the notes-plus-audiotapes method.

On the other hand, suppose you are planning to make a high-stakes decision and will use the focus group findings to supplement information from other sources. In this case, you may not be as concerned about the completeness of the focus group findings. Here, you might choose either the notes-only method or the notes-plus-audiotapes method as a more practical alternative. Furthermore, if you use the focus groups for purposes that will not lead to high-stakes decisions (for example, identifying ideas for an upcoming school fund-raiser), then choosing a method for its practicality would certainly take precedence over choosing a method known for the completeness of findings.

What Are the Procedures for Analyzing Each Focus Group Discussion?

The second stage of the analysis process pertains to analyzing each focus group discussion separately. During this stage of analysis, you must work with only one focus group at a time—and should finish analyzing the information from one discussion before proceeding to analyze another. Each focus group will be analyzed according to the method you selected for information identification: typed transcript, audiotapes, notes plus audio-tapes, or notes only. The mechanics of actually analyzing each focus group discussion is explained in a step-by-step manner in the box on pages 116 and 117.

Identifying Relevant Information. Analyzing each focus group discussion begins with the task of identifying relevant information for each of the main questions from that focus group. That "information" you identify could be a phrase, a sentence or two, or a paragraph. But regardless of whether it is a phrase or an entire paragraph, how does one decide what information is relevant and what is not? That decision rests on whether a particular piece of information directly relates to the purpose of your project. In other words, does the information provide an answer to the question inherent in your stated purpose? If the information does provide an answer, then identify it for analysis; if it does not, then do not identify or analyze it. Just set the in-formation aside. For example, look at the lines 11 through 15 of the sample transcript in the box on page 118. Now, consider whether that information is directly relevant to the purpose of this project, which was to identify com-munication problems between home and school. Because that information ad-dresses a possible solution (setting convenient conference times) rather than a problem, it is not directly relevant and is not identified as such. In contrast, the information in lines 16 to 23 does describe a home-school com-munication problem; therefore that information is identified as relevant.

Please note, the goal here is to identify the main point from what is said rather than to identify every word that is said about it. During a conversa-tion, people often take a while to "get to the point." When you listen to an audiotape or read a transcript of a focus group discussion, you will cer-tainly notice that conversational language is sprinkled with half-finished sentences, repeated phrases, unnecessary details, and so on. For example, in lines 24 through 29 of the sample transcript in the box on page 118, the participant continues to expand on the main point stated earlier. However, what is said here is not essential to the main point and is not identified as relevant information.

As you determine the relevance of a participant's comment, you will also decide whether the relevant information would make a good quota-tion. You will make this decision based on the degree to which the partici-pant's comment clearly illustrates a relevant main point identified in the focus group discussion. At this stage in the analysis, you will really only identify possible quotations; the final decision regarding which of them to eventually use as part of a report will be made during the third stage of analysis.

Sometimes, deciding which information is relevant is not always as clear-cut as we might wish. In these cases, we recommend that you consult with another person involved in the project before making the final deci-sion about whether to identify a particular piece of information as relevant or to set it aside. Also, you may sometimes find yourself hesitating to set aside some information that seems worthwhile even though it may not

Stage 2: Analyzing Each Focus Group

Typed Transcript

1. Transcribe the audiotapes. Remember to make a copy of the audiotape before parting with it.
2. Prepare and print the transcript. When preparing the transcript, use a 3" to 3½" right margin so the text is on the left half of the page. The right half of the page can be used to write notes. See page 118 for a sample transcript page.
3. Read through the transcript and mark (bracket or highlight) all relevant information, including quotes, for each question. See page 118.
4. Paraphrase and condense the information identified by the bracketing or highlighting. Write the paraphrased and condensed information on the blank right half of the page next to the bracketed or highlighted section.
5. Place the condensed information under the main question to which it applies by cutting and pasting all that information. This cut-and-paste activity can be done on a word processor or by manually cutting and pasting the transcript. If it is done manually, remember to make a copy of the transcript before cutting it apart.
6. Check the information compiled for each question against the summaries at the end of each question in the transcript and against the post-focus-group summary to ensure that it is accurate and that no key points have been missed.

Audiotapes

1. Start the process by writing each question on a separate page.
2. Listen to the tape and jot down all relevant information (including quotations) for the first question. Here, you will do the following three tasks concurrently:

   - Listen to the tape and identify relevant information
   - Mentally paraphrase and condense that information
   - Write down the paraphrased, condensed information on the page designated for that question

   If you do not prefer to note down answers while listening to the tape, another option is to record all the relevant information on another tape, using a two-deck tape recorder, or on a Dictaphone. After recording all the answers, transcribe the audiotape.
3. Check the information you write down for the first question against the end-of-the-question summary you hear in the tape.
4. Repeat Steps 2 and 3 for the subsequent questions.
5. Check the information you compile under each question against the post-focus-group summary to ensure that it is accurate and that

no key points are being missed. Exclude or include information as needed. Remember, if you record the key points and get the record transcribed, you will also have to check the compiled information against the end-of-the-question summaries you hear in the tape.

Notes Plus Audiotapes
1. Start the process by writing each question on a separate page.
2. Identify the relevant information for each question from the notes.
3. Either copy or manually cut and paste the relevant information on the page designated for that question.
4. Ascertain the accuracy and completeness of the compiled information by checking it against the post-focus-group summary. Include or exclude information as needed.
5. Listen to the tape and write down all the quotations that illustrate the main points in the findings.

Notes Only
1. Start the process by writing each question on a separate page.
2. Identify the relevant information for each question from the notes.
3. Either copy or manually cut and paste the relevant information on the page for the question to which it applies.
4. Ascertain the accuracy and completeness of the compiled information by checking it against the post-focus-group summary. Include or exclude information as needed.

directly relate to your project. In such cases, be aware that by setting aside information, you are not necessarily making a decision about its overall importance. In all likelihood, you will set aside some information that, although important, does not relate directly to the current project. However, that important but unused information is not really "lost." It may well stay in the back of your mind and inform and influence other decisions. Or, some information you have not used in the current project may alert you to another issue for which you will need additional information.

Paraphrase and Condense the Identified Information. Even though you have set aside a good bit of the information produced by the focus group, the amount of information you have identified is still substantial. Therefore for this remaining information to be usable, you must paraphrase and condense it. For example, look again at lines 16 through 23 in the sample transcript on page 118. The information in those lines has been condensed into a much smaller paraphrased version as written in the right margin. (If you are using the notes-only or notes-plus-audiotapes methods, most of your notes may already be paraphrased as main points.)

Sample Transcript Page

Purpose of the focus group project: to identify the home-school communication problems

1 2 3 4	Okay, because teachers aren't given time, aren't given release time during the day to come back in the evening. Is that what you are saying so that if it's an option a lot of people just aren't going to do it?	
5 6 7 8 9 10	It does create a lot of problems. [You have people who teach in junior colleges in the evenings, you have people who have other . . . For example sometimes they . . . In Snyderville they'd schedule parent/teacher conferences when I had a city council meeting.] What am I supposed to do?	*Teachers' other commitments are in conflict with the evening conferences, e.g., teach in college*
11 12 13 14 15 16 17 18 19 20 21 22 23 24 25 26 27 28 29	You know with the idea I think it's a great idea and I think you want to try to set conference times that are convenient and flexible for working parents. I mean it's an admirable thing to do. Many schools have done it. They would do it once a year but in the specific case like ours [we do ours on a Thursday evening when Thursday afternoon teachers go home and then we have conferences Friday morning. Well, parents who would like, because Friday is only a half day or kids aren't in school Friday, they don't want conference on Friday even though they are available so they'll take up the Thursday night times which some people who can only come then can't get in.] And usually the student to see, the parents are a little slow in getting the forms in, everything is filled up so I mean it's a great idea, and I wish we had the flexibility and professionalism to say to any teacher at any time you're going to schedule a conference with three of your parents tonight, great, I'll cover your classes, go home for the afternoon.	*Number of evening slots is insufficient for parents who want or need them*

Place Condensed Information Under Main Questions. This is essentially a cut-and-paste activity when you are working with a typed transcript. On the other hand, if you are working with an audiotape, this step will be completed at the same time you paraphrase and condense the information. That is, you will write each paraphrase directly onto the page for the question to which it applies. When working only with notes, you could choose to either recopy or manually cut each main point from your notes onto the page for the question to which it applies. The final step, whichever method you are using, is to recheck your work to ensure that no key points have been missed. You can do this by checking the compiled information against the post-focus-group summary. If you are working with an audiotape or transcript, you can also check the compiled information against the summaries after each main question.

Transcribing and Transcribers: Some Tips

- Although anyone can attempt to transcribe the audiotapes, please note that it is not an easy task. An experienced transcriber needs an average of 4 to 5 hours to transcribe an hour of tape. This time varies depending on the quality of the recording and the clarity of participants' comments.
- You can locate a transcriber by looking in the Yellow Pages under "Transcribing Services," "Secretarial Services," or by advertising in local newspapers (including community college or university papers). Current transcriber rates are at least $20 per hour.
- When interviewing potential transcribers, ask the following questions:

Have you transcribed focus group discussions, group interviews, or meetings?

Do you transcribe regular cassettes or microcassettes?

How much do you charge per hour?

Is there an additional charge per page?

Is there an additional charge for copies on disk?

What is your turnaround time for each audiotaped focus group discussion?

How many words do you type per minute from an audiotape?

How much time do you typically need to transcribe an hour of audiotape?

How many pages of manuscript are usually produced for that hour?

Do you give a copy on disk, on paper, or both?

How are transcribed pages formatted (e.g., margins, font size)?

How many focus group discussions—or group interviews—have you transcribed? May I have those names as references?

- If you are planning on using in-house secretarial help to transcribe the focus groups, it would be prudent to invest in transcribing equipment. The task of transcribing becomes easier if you have transcribing equipment that will help you in controlling the speed and tone of the recorded tape and in rewinding and forwarding the tape by means of foot pedals. You can look for sources that sell transcribing equipment by looking in the Yellow Pages or on the Internet. The key words are "Dictation Equipment" or "Transcribing Equipment." You can expect to pay approximately $250 to $450 for the transcribing equipment.

What Are the Procedures for Analyzing and Interpreting Findings From All the Focus Groups?

At this point in the analysis process, you will be combining information within each participant group (Stage 3), comparing and contrasting information across participant groups (Stage 4), and interpreting information from the entire project (Stage 5). With respect to Stage 3, information within each participant group (e.g., parents, teachers, or students) can be combined in the following manner:

- First, collate the information from all focus groups that have the same participant group. For example, let's say that in Stage 2, you analyzed three focus groups separately—each composed of parents. Now, you have to collate the findings from all three parent focus groups into one pile.
- Next, organize the information so that the information from all those focus groups is placed together under each main question.
- Finally, read through the reorganized information present under each main question and determine whether you need categories to group that information. Categories can be considered as headings to organize the information or as themes that are evident from the gathered information. After determining any categories, group the reorganized information under each main question into categories and subcategories as needed. To understand this process better, consider the example of the three parent groups again. Let's say one of the main questions for these parent focus groups was, "What communication problems exist between home and school?" The information from the three parent focus groups that was organized under this question is now grouped into the following two categories: (a) communication problems due to lack of time and opportunity and (b) communication problems due to differing parent-teacher perceptions. In the analysis of your own focus group project, you will no doubt find the categorization task difficult at times. For example, sometimes the main point of participants' comments may not be clear even though the moderator has effectively probed. There is no quick and easy solution for these difficulties. Nevertheless, we remind you that the task here is to categorize according to the participant's meaning (as best you can discern it), communicated by the words themselves rather than "reading into it" your interpretation of what was meant.

In Stage 4, information from the various participant groups is compared and contrasted. Here, read through the combined information from each participant group and write down similarities and differences across these participant groups for each category under each main question. Then, in the final stage of analysis (Stage 5), findings from the entire focus group project are interpreted. Here, read through the analysis and reflect on the findings that are particularly salient in light of the purpose of the project. You then describe what the findings mean in terms of the questions inherent in that purpose. You should also describe how the focus group findings could or should influence any pending decisions.

What Should Be Included in a Focus Group Report?

A focus group report must be prepared if there is a need for reporting the findings of the focus group project in writing. The focus group report should include at least the following three sections:

- Project description
- Findings
- Summary and implications

On pages 123 and 124, a partial report is presented to illustrate what should be included in the section on project description. In the "Findings" and "Summary and Implications" sections of this partial report, you will note that an outline or bulleting format is used. We recommend an outline rather than a narrative form for reports because we believe it is more suited to school situations. Outlining makes for a report that is more easily written and subsequently more easily read. Formatting a report in this style takes less time and effort to prepare than a narrative report. This is certainly an important advantage given the time constraints of school personnel. For the readers of the report, an outline format is more concise and the essential content stands out. In contrast, a narrative report would be lengthier and the key points of the report would be imbedded within the paragraphs.

In addition to determining the format of the report, you will also be determining how to word the content. As you do so, keep in mind that a focus group report is essentially a verbal description of participants' attitudes and opinions. Numerical description—numbers or percentages—are not appropriate for focus group reports. However, it is acceptable to use words such as *all, most, many, some, few,* and *none* in the reports to provide a sense of how often particular comments were voiced.

The sample report on pages 123 and 124 is a partial example of a report intended to present a more complete and detailed picture. However, you may instead choose to write a briefer report that is no more than two pages long. While you may not need all the detail, you would still want to convey all the essential information and the important highlights of the focus group project. If this is your goal, use the following guidelines to develop that report:

Cross-Reference Tip
To learn more about why numerical descriptions are not appropriate for focus group reports, please see Chapter 1, pages 5-6.

- For project description, include only the purpose of the project, the various participant groups, and the project leader and/or contact person.
- For findings, present the most salient features of the project as a bulleted list. (Exclude quotations; also exclude questions, categories, and subcategories as needed.)
- For summaries and implications in a nutshell, write a concise answer to the following question: "What did I learn from the project that is the most important, and how will that affect my decisions?"

When Is a Written Analysis or Report Unnecessary?

In the final section of this chapter, we would like to call attention to some instances when written analyses or reports for focus group projects are not needed. But first, a note of caution: The lack of a written analysis or report does not mean that no one need analyze the information or record the salient points of the discussion. It means that the information from the focus group discussion is being processed mentally and the salient features of the focus group discussion are being recorded in the form of rough notes.

Broadly speaking, written analyses or reports are not necessary in the following instances:

- When one or two focus groups are conducted and decisions or changes based on those focus group discussions have temporal effects (e.g., to obtain some ideas for the upcoming open house or an inservice session)
- When focus groups are conducted routinely to enable school leaders to stay "in touch" with all those concerned—teachers, parents, and students (e.g., listen and attend to their needs, problems and concerns, likes and dislikes, and feelings of satisfaction and dissatisfaction)
- When focus groups are conducted continually to improve the effectiveness of school policies, programs, and products (e.g., to determine whether the best use of teacher time is made in weekly meetings; to determine how the assignment book can be improved)

The examples above demonstrate possibilities for using focus groups that would not only render written analysis unnecessary but would also involve minimal effort to plan and conduct. Thus we return to a point made in the first chapter of this book: We challenged you to view the examples provided throughout this book as merely a starting point for considering a wide range of possible uses for focus groups in your own situation. This range of uses would include occasions in which you have no particular

Sample Report

[The following section describes the project's purpose.]

Project Description
- *Purpose:* The purpose of the project is to identify communication problems between home and school at the elementary schools in the Snyderville School District.
- *Participant groups:* General education teachers and parents
- *Number of focus groups per participant group:* Three groups of general education teachers and three groups of parents
- *Number of participants per participant group:* 21 general education teachers and 19 parents
- *When were the focus groups conducted?* September 2000
- *Project leader/contact person:* Mary Wood

[The following section describes some of the findings—that is, those relating mainly to general education teachers. Note how the question, categories, and subcategories have been used to present the information. A complete section on the findings would include additional information on parent perceptions.]

Findings

Question: What communication problems have you faced or are you facing?

Communication Problems

Teachers and parents identified similar homework-communication problems. However, they differed as far as who they thought was responsible for these problems:
- Not initiating communication with each other
- Not communicating often enough with each other
- Not communicating regularly enough with each other
- Not communicating early enough with each other
- Not following through with what they have said they will do to communicate with each other
- Not communicating in a clear and useful manner with each other

Factors Contributing to the Communication Problems as Identified by General Education Teachers

Communication problems arising from lack of time and opportunity:
- Teachers' work schedules do not permit them to contact the parents during the school day.

(continued)

- Teachers have a lot of paperwork and record keeping to do; this takes time away from communication.
- Teachers have heavy student caseloads and do not have enough time to communicate with all the parents regularly.

"I have sent 5 notes and left 3 messages. I haven't heard from the parent yet. What more can I do? I have 25 other children to attend to."

"I would like to communicate with my parents more often. But how? I am unable to do it during school. After going home, I have my own family to take care of and of course papers to grade."

Communication problems relating to telephone calls:
- Teachers find it difficult to make calls from school because telephones are not present in their classrooms, an open line is not easily available, long-distance calls are not possible, and/or families have no phone.
- Teachers find it difficult to receive calls at school because they cannot be reached easily by phone and/or phone messages get delayed or lost.

"We don't have telephones in classrooms. And even if we did, I cannot keep answering the phone. I end up playing telephone tag with the parents. By the time we touch base, it is too late."

"Many of our parents do not have a telephone and even if they do, I have trouble communicating because I do not speak their language."

[The following section is a partial description of the summarizations and implications.]

Summary and Implications
- Both teachers and parents are "at fault." Neither of them initiate communication, follow through, or communicate early on.
- The mode of communication needs to be addressed. It is hard for parents to keep track of the paper trail.
- Teachers have to be more accessible to the parents.
- It is clear that the onus of responsibility for better communication rests on both teachers and parents. What can we do to make both parties more responsible and accountable?
- Additional focus groups could be conducted to generate solutions for addressing these problems.

decision in mind other than to stay informed about school matters on a continuing basis. In reality, using focus groups could inform you for the incremental decisions you make every day without much conscious thought, such as how to interact with parents, students, and the community. These "little" decisions probably have at least as much impact as the bigger decisions do on morale and continual improvement of school programs, policies, and products. At the other end of the range of possible uses, there will be times when a far-reaching decision is on the table, a common example being a decision about school funding referenda. In such a case, focus groups could provide information that would be absolutely essential for assessing consumer support or planning how to gain that support. For this and other situations, we hope this book has given you the tools to use focus groups in ways that are meaningful, useful, and practical.

At a Glance:
Analyzing and Reporting Focus Group Findings

❏ Have I determined the need for written analysis or report?

If a written analysis or report *is* needed,
❏ Have I determined who will analyze the focus group information?
❏ Have I determined which method of identifying relevant information is to be used?
❏ If it is the transcript method, have I transcribed the audiotapes and prepared the transcripts?
❏ Have I analyzed each focus group discussion separately?
❏ Have I combined information *within* each participant group?
❏ Have I compared and contrasted information *across* participant groups?
❏ Have I interpreted the information from the entire focus group project?
❏ Have I determined whether I need a detailed or a brief report?
❏ Have I written the report?

If a written analysis or report is *not* needed,
❏ Have I mentally processed the information gathered from the focus group discussions?
❏ Have I made rough notes of the salient points?

References

Advertising Research Foundation. (1985). *Focus groups: Issues and approaches.* New York: Advertising Research Foundation.

Axelrod, M. D. (1975, March 14). 10 essentials for good qualitative research. *Marketing News,* 10-11.

Beck, L. C., Trombetta, W. L., & Share, C. (1986). Using focus group sessions before decisions are made. *North Carolina Medical Journal, 47*(2), 73-74.

Bellenger, D. N., Bernhardt, K. L., & Goldstucker, J. L. (1976). Qualitative research techniques: Focus group interviews. In *Qualitative Research in Marketing* (pp. 7-28). Chicago: American Marketing Association.

Berard, Y. (1998, December 23). Carroll's bond plans shaping up. *Fort Worth Star-Telegram,* p. M1.

Bolton, M. (2000, February 9). School board weighs feedback. *Times Union,* p. F1.

Broom, G. M., & Dozier, D. M. (1990). *Using public relations research: Applications to program management.* Englewood Cliffs, NJ: Prentice Hall.

Campbell, G. (1992, June 18). Consultant travels in many worlds. *Wisconsin State Journal,* p. 1F.

Chalifoux, J. M. (1997, June 13). Berlin-Boylston detail ideal superintendent. *Telegram & Gazette,* p. B2.

Erkut, S., & Fields, J. P. (1987). Focus groups to the rescue. *Training and Development Journal, 41*(10), 74-76.

Fern, E. F. (1982). The use of focus groups for idea generation: The effects of group size, acquaintanceship, and moderator on response quantity and quality. *Journal of Marketing Research, 19,* 1-13.

Focus groups planned on school costs. (1993, January 8). *Capital Times,* p. 2B.

Gaynair, G. (1995, November 8). Webb tops field for troubled Fairborn Schools. *Dayton Daily News,* p. 7A.

Gerry, S. (2000, November 4). Olathe School District has wrapped up focus groups on high schools. *Kansas City Star,* p. 1.

Grunig, L. A. (1990). Using focus group research in public relations. *Public Relations Review, 16*(2), 36-49.

Guerard, M. B. (2000, February 16). Groups find different school focuses, audit shows. *Post and Courier,* p. 1B.

Hayward, W., & Rose, J. (1995). "We'll meet again . . ."; Repeat attendance at group discussions—does it matter? *Journal of Market Research Society, 32*(3), 377-407.

Johnson, J. (1995, February 24). School officials debate failed referendum issues. *Chicago Daily Herald,* p. 10, News.

Karger, T. (1987, August 28). Focus groups are for focusing and for little else. *Marketing News*, 52-55.

Krueger, R. A. (1994). *Focus groups: A practical guide for applied research* (2nd ed.). Thousand Oaks, CA: Sage.

Levy, S. J. (1979). Focus group interviewing. In J. B. Higginbotham & K. K. Cox (Eds.), *Focus group interviews: A reader* (pp. 29-37). Chicago: American Marketing Association.

Merton, R. K., Fiske, M., & Kendall, P. (1956). *The focused interview.* Glencoe, IL: Free Press.

Nelson, J. S., & Coe, E. (2000). [The role of focus groups in school decision making: Media reports over 2 decades]. Unpublished raw data.

Olathe District 21st-Century High School Steering Team. (2001). *Envisioning 21st-century programming: A process for change* (Phase I—Focus Group Executive Summary). Olathe, KS: Olathe School District.

Parents look to keep gifted programs. (1993, December 8). *Plain Dealer*, p. 5C.

Post Falls seeks input on filling job. (2000, December 5). *Spokesman-Review*, p. B2.

Russell, S. (1995, September 29). Schools turn to focus groups for insight. *Capital Times*, p. 3A.

Scruggs, A. E. (1994, June 22). Lakewood schools hire levy consultant. *Plain Dealer*, p. 7B.

Sevier, R. (1989, Winter). Conducting focus group research. *Journal of College Admissions, 122*, 4-9.

Vaughn, S., Schumm, J. S., & Sinagub, J. (1996). *Focus group interviews in education and psychology.* Thousand Oaks, CA: Sage.

Waller, C. L. (1995, February 24). Residents' input sought on Dist. 128 overcrowding. *Chicago Daily Herald*, p. 1L.

Washington, W. (1994, November 23). Racial tolerance crumbling in the halls: School study details problem. *Star Tribune*, p. 1A.

Weitzman, E. A., & Miles, M. B. (1995). *Computer programs for qualitative data analysis.* Thousand Oaks, CA: Sage.

Wells, W. D. (1974). Group interviewing. In R. Ferber (Ed.), *Handbook of Marketing Research* (pp. 133-146). New York: McGraw-Hill.

Wheatley, K. L., & Flexner, W. A. (May 9, 1988). Dimensions that make focus groups work. *Marketing News*, 16-17.

Index

CORWIN
PRESS

The Corwin Press logo—a raven striding across an open book—represents the happy union of courage and learning. We are a professional-level publisher of books and journals for K-12 educators, and we are committed to creating and providing resources that embody these qualities. Corwin's motto is "Success for All Learners."